presents

Maha Reiki® Level 2 Manual

In Depth Reiki Training for Our Times

Donna Lambdin, Ph.D.
Ron Goodwin, Ph.D.

For online training webinar information, please visit www.mahamethods.com

ACKNOWLEDGMENTS

Donna wishes to thank her guardian angel who is referred to as Grandmother, for reminding her of her sacred contract. This manual is in part the fulfillment of that contract. Donna also wants to express her gratitude to Lorrie Richmond for introducing her to Reiki and for being a wonderful friend and confidant. She also wants to thank her mentor Rosalie and her Reiki Master Teachers for their teachings, patience, and wisdom.

Many others have helped us on our journey, especially our Kundalini Yoga Instructor Shamsher.

We thank Barbara DuBois for the cover design and page layout, along with her graphic illustrations; Lisa Lombardo for her cover and chapter header artwork; and Cori Johnson for helping us with our computers and technology.

The support and encouragement from our friends, students, clients, fellow Reiki Masters and Practitioners has been most helpful.

It was our privilege to meet an incredible artist while we were in Kona, Hawaii: Francene Hart. She has allowed us to use a few of her prints in our manual. For this we are forever grateful. Her website is *www.francenehart.com* and her mailing address is P.O. Box 900, Honaunau, HI 96726.

So much Love, Light, and Blessings to all on your Reiki journey.

Donna Lambdin and Ron Goodwin

DISCLAIMER

The purpose of this training manual is to assist Maha Reiki® Master Teachers and their students in understanding and learning Maha Reiki®. Maha Reiki® cannot be learned and practiced without receiving an attunement from a qualified Maha Reiki® Master Teacher.

The information in this manual is not medical advice and is not intended as a substitute for seeking medical attention.

Copyright ©2017 by Donna Lambdin, Ph.D. and Ronald Goodwin, Ph.D.

All rights reserved. No part of this manual may reproduced in whole, in part, or in any form without the written consent of the authors.

TABLE OF CONTENTS

Foreword 1

Code of Ethics 2

Welcome Letter 3

Illustration: Master Lineage 5

Five Precepts 6

Illustration: *Wheels of Light* by Francene Hart 7

Chakra Balancing Meditation 9

Illustration: Spinning Chakras 11

Illustration: Auric Field Layers 12

Auric Field 13

Aura Strengthening Exercise 15

Illustration: *Receiving* by Francene Hart 17

Meditation for Attunement, Level 2 19

The Level 2 Reiki Symbols 20

Symbols Description 21

Cho Ku Rei – Power Symbol 24

Sei Heki – Mental/Emotional Symbol 27

Hon Sha Ze Sho Nen – Long Distance Symbol 30

Illustration: *Earth Prayer* by Francene Hart 33

Exercises for Symbols 35

Illustration: Symbol Diagrams 37

Sending Reiki With the Eyes 39

Sending Reiki With the Breath 40

Sending Reiki Long Distance 42

Weaving with *Cho Ku Rei* 44

Illustration: *Cho Ku Rei* Symbol on the Body 46

Planting Stars and Running Light 47

Illustration: Anatomy for Reiki (Front View) 48

Illustration: Anatomy for Reiki (Back View) 49

Illustration: Circulation Glow 50
Louise Hay 51
Masaru Emoto 52
Mantras 53
Crystals 56
Reiki Healing Grids 57
Flower of Life/Sacred Geometry 59
Illustration: Flower of Life Grid 60
Photograph: Crystal Grid 61
Antahkarana 63
Illustration: Antahkarana 65
MerKaBa 67
Illustration: MerKaBa Grid 69
Daily Practice 71
Sacred Space 73
Reiki Circle 74
Client Information Form 75
Bibliography 77

FOREWORD

The time is now!

In this current time of conscious development, fresh tools for teaching and learning are needed to assist in this journey. Many books have been written on Reiki, energetic, vibrational, and spiritual healing. Current mainstream magazines have recently published articles on a variety of alternative energetic healing methods, thus bringing the awareness of these methods to the public eye. The overview of these articles is sparking interest and awakening many people.

As individuals begin to awaken, many feel lost as to where to begin to find answers. The internet provides an immense amount of information, but where does a person go to find actual training? Hands on instruction is needed for Reiki and many other alternative healing methods. Many attunements and empowerments, unlocking the keys to raise vibrational consciousness, are passed on from teacher to student, in person.

Understanding, experiencing, and continuing guidance and support are important when a person is just beginning and continues to practice Reiki. Person to person contact fulfills this movement and growth. Contact with your Reiki Master Teacher and other Reiki practitioners can be extremely supportive and comforting.

Maha Reiki® has developed over many years of practicing and teaching the Usui and Tibetan styles of Reiki. These teachings are the foundation of this practice. Maha is a Sanskrit word meaning "Great". New methods and ways of understanding the power of this amazing Reiki energy have grown and developed with daily practice and sessions with countless clients and students. "Do not minimize," these were the words spoken to me by Spirit. This guidance has assisted in my growth, continuing development, understanding, and teaching others advanced techniques with the Maha Reiki® energy.

This Maha Reiki® Level 2 manual provides more advanced techniques and methods to empower and support the growth of your Reiki practice. This manual does not replace the need for the student to receive an in-person attunement from a qualified Maha Reiki® Master Teacher.

The time is now! Unlock your energetic, infinite potential!
Many blessings on your journey!

Donna Lambdin
Maha Reiki® Master Teacher

MAHA REIKI®
CODE OF ETHICS

The following are the basic operating principles of Maha Reiki® and our Code of Ethics. All students, practitioners, and teachers should keep these principles in mind as they practice and teach Maha Reiki®.

1. Show gratitude for the gift of Reiki and for all fellow students, practitioners, and teachers, regardless of school or lineage.

2. Be honest, show respect, and have integrity in all you do.

3. Treat all information from clients, students, practitioners, and teachers in a confidential manner.

4. Recognize that Reiki works in conjunction with other forms of medical care. Never diagnose or prescribe medications. Refer clients other health care professionals when appropriate.

5. Always act in a professional manner and maintain a professional image.

6. Use common sense and seek the advice of experienced Maha Reiki® professionals when in doubt.

Welcome to Maha Reiki® Level 2 Training!

Your journey continues to lead you into living, breathing, embracing and growing into higher vibration. This second level of Maha Reiki® training will bring gifts of greater tools of higher energy to assist you and others in vibrational healing.

Learning the names and how to draw the healing symbols greatly enhances their powerful healing energy and Divine connection. Daily practice and activation allows their energy to grow more and more powerful, raising your own personal vibration to greater, unbounded heights. Remember, you grow as much as you can each day and do not minimize your potential!!!

Your talents and gifts will continue to unfold to higher and higher potential. Trust, practice, just for today...grow, heal, open your heart chakra to greater and greater compassion. Love, unconditional love flowing through us, carrying the healing for the highest good.

Welcome to this class. Walking this journey with you is a great honor. The energy and support of Community continues to grow worldwide, with infinite light and love...Exciting!!!

Sat Nam, Namaste,
Donna Lambdin
Maha Reiki® Master Teacher

Master Lineage

Dr. Mikao Usui

Kan'ichi Taketomi

Dr. Chujiro Hayashi

Kimiko Koyama
Hiroshi Doi

Chiyoko Yamaguchi
Hyakuten Inamoto

Mrs. Hawayo Takata

Iris Ishikura
Arthur Robertson
Diane McCumber

Iris Ishikura
Arthur Robertson
Marlene Schilke

Phyllis Lei Furumoto
Carol Farmer
Leah Smith

Helen Haberlay
Mary Ellen Floyd

William Lee Rand
Colleen Benelli

Donna Lambdin

Ron Goodwin

THE FIVE PRECEPTS

Usui Sensei taught his students to place their hands together at their heart, morning and night, and repeat five precepts/principles. There are several similar interpretations of these precepts.
The following are the ones we are drawn to chant:

Just for today release anger

Just for today release worries

Earn your living honestly

Express gratitude

Be kind to every living thing

Repeating these precepts out loud, from your heart, can remind you, bring you joy in the moment, and carry you through your day with love!

CHAKRA BALANCING MEDITATION

Sit comfortably with your spine as straight as possible, your feet flat on the floor or legs in easy pose.

Place your hands in Gassho, thumbs touching your heart.

Close your eyes. Take a few long slow deep breaths and slowly exhale out any tension or tightness. Relax the muscles around your ribs and any other area that may be constricting a full breath.

In your mind's eye, visualize and connect with the Earth Star, beneath your feet.

Feel your crown opening, connecting through your Crown and Star chakras to your highest mind, Cosmos, Divine infinite connection, brightest light from Source.

Slowly, starting from the Earth chakra, bring your long deep breath from the Earth through your entire body, to your light connection. Repeat three to five times.

When you feel relaxed, on your next breath up, chant LAM. Relax your chin. Open your mouth, do not clench your lips or teeth. Feel this long note vibrate your Root chakra for the entire breath. Repeat at least three times. Continue until you feel your Root chakra vibrating.

Once your Root chakra is vibrating, move up to your Sacral chakra.
Keep your chin relaxed and your spine straight. Feel the Earth chakra beneath your feet and your Crown and Star chakra opening to even greater amounts of Divine light flowing from the Cosmos.
Long deep breath, chant VAM. Feel your Sacral chakra vibrating with the long exhalation.
Repeat at least three times. Continue until you feel your Sacral chakra vibrating.
Now feel your Root and Sacral chakras vibrating together with the next breath.
Repeat this breath at least three times. Continue until you feel them spinning together.

Once you feel these two chakras spinning together, move up to your Solar Plexus chakra.
Keep your chin relaxed and your spine straight. Feel the Earth chakra beneath your feet and your Crown and Star chakra opening to even greater amounts of Divine light flowing from the Cosmos.
Long deep breath, chant RAM. Feel your Solar Plexus chakra vibrating with the long exhalation.
Repeat this breath at least three times. Continue until you feel your Solar Plexus chakra vibrating.
Now feel your Root, Sacral and Solar Plexus chakras vibrating together with the next breath.
Repeat this breath at least three times. Continue until you feel them spinning together.

Once you feel these three chakras spinning together, move up to your Heart chakra.
Keep your chin relaxed and your spine straight. Feel the Earth chakra beneath your feet and your Crown and Star chakra opening to even greater amounts of Divine light flowing from the Cosmos.
Long deep breath, chant YAM. Feel your Heart chakra vibrating with the long exhalation.

Repeat at least three times. Continue until you feel your Heart chakra vibrating. Feel the Heart growing, expanding with greater volumes of sound moving up from your lower chakras and more light flowing down from the Cosmos. Visualize your Heart as a glowing, growing, radiant expanding star.
Now feel your Root, Sacral, Solar Plexus, and Heart chakras vibrating together with the next breath. Repeat this breath at least three times. Continue until you feel them spinning together.

Once you feel these four chakras spinning together, move up to your Throat chakra.
Keep your chin relaxed and your spine straight. Feel the Earth chakra beneath your feet and your Crown and Star chakra opening to even greater amounts of Divine light flowing from the Cosmos.
Long deep breath, chant HAM. Feel your Throat chakra vibrating with the long exhalation. Feel the physical throat opening and expanding, allowing a greater volume of sound to vibrate through.
Repeat at least three times. Continue until you feel your Throat chakra fully open and vibrating.
Now feel your Root, Sacral, Solar Plexus, Heart, and Throat chakras vibrating together with the next longer, deeper breath. Repeat this breath at least three times. Continue until you feel them spinning together.

Once you feel these five chakras spinning together, move up to your Third Eye chakra.
Keep your chin relaxed and your spine straight. Feel the Earth chakra beneath your feet and your Crown and Star chakra opening to even greater amounts of Divine light flowing from the Cosmos.
Long deep breath, chant OM. Feel your Third Eye chakra vibrating with the long exhalation. Feel the pineal and pituitary glands, behind your Third Eye, opening and expanding, allowing a greater volume of light and sound to vibrate through. Repeat at least three times. Continue until you feel your Third Eye chakra fully open and vibrating. Now feel your Root, Sacral, Solar Plexus, Heart, Throat, and Third Eye chakras vibrating together with the next longer, deeper breath. Repeat this breath at least three times. Continue until you feel them spinning together.

Once you feel these six chakras spinning together, move up to your Crown chakra.
Keep your chin relaxed and your spine straight. Feel the Earth chakra beneath your feet and your Crown and Star chakra opening to even greater amounts of Divine light flowing from the Cosmos.
Long deep breath, slowly exhale. Feel your Crown chakra vibrating and opening to even greater volumes of cosmic light flowing, with the long exhalation. Feel the pineal and pituitary glands, behind your Third Eye, opening and expanding more, allowing a greater volume of light to flow through.
Repeat at least three times. Continue until you feel your Crown chakra fully open and vibrating.
Now feel your Root, Sacral, Solar Plexus, Heart, Throat, Third Eye, and Crown chakras vibrating and flowing together with the next longer, deeper breath. Repeat this breath at least three times. Continue until you feel them spinning together.

With your seven chakras spinning together, connected to your Earth and Star chakras, feel the movement and opening of your central channel. You now have a direct connection to infinite, Divine Light from Source and a grounding with the Mother Earth. You may experience a feeling of pure joy, euphoria, see colors, feel or see your Light Guides, or have many other amazing experiences.

Relax with your hands on your thighs, palms facing up in the receiving gesture, mudra.

Being connected and in balance is an opportune time to enjoy being completely relaxed, ask for guidance, release emotions or trauma, journey, etc, or just "BE."

SPINNING CHAKRAS

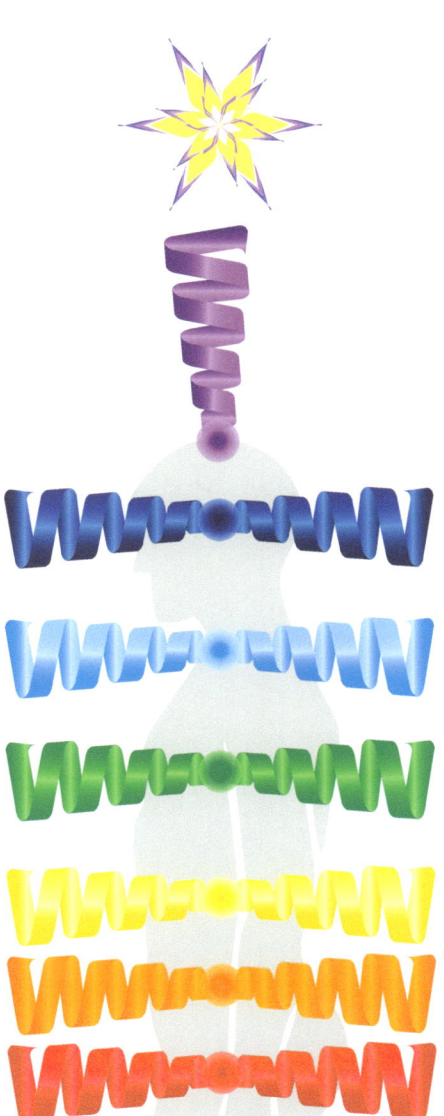

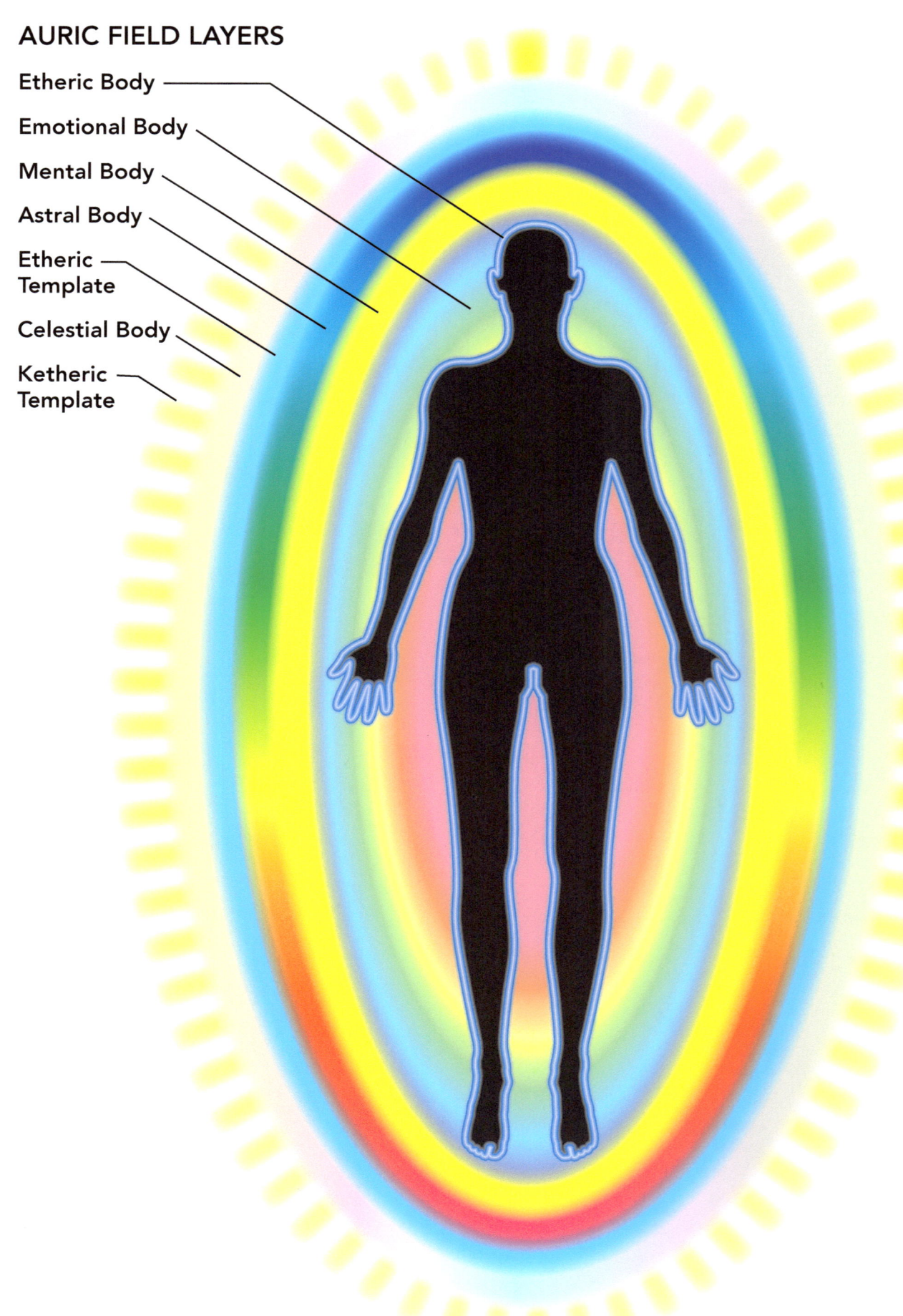

AURIC FIELD

The auric field is important to discuss since it is an interconnected field of energetic layers or *subtle bodies* around the physical body. These layers are connected to the body via energy points commonly known as *chakras*.

The auric field is known as a holographic energetic template, or the biomagnetic field that surrounds our physical body. This field can be detected and seen by psychics, some energetic healers, and photographed with Kirlian photography.

Cyndi Dale, in her book *New Chakra Healing: The Revolutionary 32-Center Energy System* (1998), explains the connection between the chakra system and the auric field: "Many psychics differentiate the esoteric bodies this way: the aura is on the outside of the body; the chakras are on the inside. Though this theory can conceptually help us, it does not tell the entire story. Nature doesn't really differentiate between the insides and outsides of things. The truth is, the chakras are holistic units that tie into, interact with, and help form the auric layers. These auric layers are also holistic units. The aura as a whole includes the chakras and every other aspect of our being. It is also a sub-unit of our energetic self because its major functions enable us to interact with our external environment and the physical, mental, emotional, and spiritual dimensions that are constantly at play with our being" (134).

The auric field is your first line of defense and protection. It is a highly effective shield against external forces. Because it is not well known, especially in the western world, it has not received care. Just as we must daily care for all parts of our body, we must also daily take care of our auric field. The auric field can expand up to nine feet when healthy. It is composed of seven subtle, energetic, multidimensional layers. Each layer increases in higher vibration as it moves away from the Physical body. It appears as an elongated sphere of light encompassing our entire physical form. Each layer can carry and reflect the colors of the in-body chakras and more. As the vibration grows, so does the shimmering glow of the colors.

The first level of the auric field is the Etheric body.

This body overlays the Physical body, expanding directly from it to about one and a half inches beyond the physical form. It carries information which guides cellular growth to the developing fetus, throughout the lifespan, and to the healthy, damaged, or diseased adult body. The Physical body cannot exist without the Etheric body. When the Etheric body is damaged or traumatized, it creates physical *dis-ease*. The Physical and Etheric bodies totally relate and speak to each other. A bluish glow is detected by Kirlian photography in this layer.

The second level of the auric field is the Emotional body.

This layer extends one to three inches beyond the Physical body. This layer is the seat of human emotions, where the "feelings" live. Emotional trauma held in this layer can cause a disruption in the vibrational rhythm of the layer, creating an imbalance to be picked up by the Etheric and transmitted to the Physical. A domino effect can be created, just as in the chakras. A rainbow of colors can be detected in this layer.

The third level of the auric field is the Mental body.

This layer extends three to eight inches beyond the Physical body. This layer holds our ideas and mental processes. Our ability to organize, disseminate information, grow beyond old programming, broaden our scope of understanding and possibilities, all reside here. The energies of being inflexible and stuck in old paradigms will flow through the Emotional and Etheric bodies to the Physical body and can create dis-ease. Yellow light can be detected in this field.

The fourth level of the auric field is the Astral body.

This layer extends about one foot beyond the Physical body. It is the bridge and doorway to spiritual connection. The Astral body is a containment vehicle for the personality beyond physical death. There is a strong association with the heart chakra. All colors may be detected here. This is where near death experiences can happen. It is also the field that psychics tap into for readings.

The fifth level of the auric field is the Etheric template.

This layer extends one to two feet beyond the Physical body. Deep blues can be detected in this layer. It is the blueprint of the physical world in another, higher vibrational dimension. The Etheric template is related to the throat chakra. Sound creates matter. Sound healing is most effective in this layer of the Auric field. The Etheric blueprint directly speaks to the Etheric body for physical, mental, emotional wellness and balance.

The sixth level of the auric field is the Celestial body.

It is associated with enlightenment and the third eye. This layer extends two to three feet beyond the Physical body. It opens access to higher knowledge and spiritual consciousness. Shimmery, pastel colors can be found in this layer. The Celestial body connects us to our purpose in life and to unconditional love. It vibrates at an extremely high level.

The seventh level of the auric field is the Ketheric template, the Causal body.

Divine and universal consciousness represent this level. This level reflects all experiences in current and previous lives. Oneness with all, connection with the Divine, is the energy present here. The Ketheric template connects directly to the crown chakra. It holds all the other layers of the auric field together. Golden rays of light flow through this layer of the auric field. These vibrations are the highest light vibration that one can experience in physical form.

Rosalyn L. Bruyere in her book, *Wheels of Light: Chakras, Auras, and the Healing Energy of the Body* (1994), summarizes the auric field: "The auric field is a metaphor for life. In other words, a person's energy field or the individual aura around the body, which is created and controlled by the chakras, reflects how one's life actually live; it mirrors the flow of that life. In this way, the auric field becomes more than a symbol for life. The aura is life" (61).

AURA STRENGTHENING EXERCISE

This exercise, when practiced with intention, fills the holes and weak areas in your auric field. The auric field is the first line of energetic defense and protection.

- Stand with your feet hip width apart and your hands resting at your sides, palms facing outward.

- Feel the earth beneath your feet.

- Raise your arms slowly, bringing the Earth energy up through all the layers of your auric field.

- Once you arrive above the top of your head, clap your hands.

- The clapping changes the vibration of what is around and within you.
(Like when a baby shakes a rattle and begins to laugh instead of cry).

- Slowly move your hands apart approximately two feet, palms still facing each other. In this position, you are receiving immense cosmic energy.

- Without stopping the flowing movement, turn your hands away from each other and slowly bring them down through all the layers of your auric field, filling them with the cosmic energy.

- As you reach the sides of your legs, slap the side of your thighs grounding this cosmic energy into your body through your feet and into the earth.

Repeat this movement many times. The more repetitions, the stronger your auric field becomes.

This movement can be done as slowly or as quickly as you desire.

Performing this movement first thing in the morning strengthens your auric field for the day.

This movement can be repeated many times a day, whenever you feel you need more strength or protection, for whatever reason.

It takes 40 days to establish a new pattern of behavior. This movement will become part of your daily practice and keep you strong and protected as you start and move through your day.

MEDITATION FOR ATTUNEMENT LEVEL 2

Sit comfortably with your back straight, feet touching the floor, and your hands, palms touching, placed at your heart chakra.

Relax the muscles around your rib cage. Feel the Earth beneath your feet.

Imagine your breath coming up from the Earth, through your feet, ankles, knees, hips, and up through all of your chakras.

As you slowly exhale, release any tension or tightness the breath has found along the way.

Continue this breath, opening and connecting all of your chakras.

Once you feel the smooth flow of breath and energy, melt into deeper relaxation. No worries, only your energy flowing and the balance of this moment is with you.

Continue to experience this flow……..

On your next breath, as you exhale, allow your crown chakra to open to even greater capacity, to receive highest light energy from your Divine Source connection.

You are now the bridge, the ladder, from Earth to the Heavens, the Cosmos.

Feel your central channel, where your chakras meet, opening wider, to receive more flowing energy from the Heavens through you to the Earth, and back up to the Heavens.

Continue with your long deep breathing, feeling brighter and brighter light flowing through your crown, circling your auric field and down through your entire body, touching every cell, flowing into the Earth and back up.

Continue to experience this connection and flow…….

Feel your heart chakra opening to greater and greater volumes of light, filling with gratitude and love.

Continue to experience this opening and growing gratitude and love…….

Completely relax every cell in your body, bathing in light.

Ask for your highest light guides and guardians to be present, as your witnesses, as you receive the gift of the Reiki 2 attunement.

THE LEVEL 2 REIKI SYMBOLS

The origin of the reiki symbols is not fully known; there are many legends and stories associated with them. These first three that you will learn today were brought down from Mount Kurama after Usui Sensei received them during his 21-day meditation. Your energetic system was infused with the symbols as you received your Level 1 Reiki training. As you gaze upon them, you will notice the energetic vibration each emits. Perhaps you will feel, or have a knowing, of how ancient they are. Because the symbols have been used for healing by millions of healers, for unknown millennia, they are extremely powerful. It is important to show reverence and respect to these ancient healing symbols. They are not secret, but sacred. Knowing their names and how to draw them greatly enhances your Reiki practice. We do not show them to others who are not Reiki trained because of their ability to begin a healing process that may not be understood or wanted at the time. Because Mrs. Takata, who is responsible for bringing Reiki training to the West, did not allow her students to write things down or leave with copies of the symbols, there are variations of them. It is important for you to memorize and imprint the symbols as your Reiki Master presents them, as this is how they will be imprinted into your energetic system.

The symbols are activated through the attunement process by a Reiki Master Teacher. The symbols are not truly activated unless this is done. There have been rare, near death instances, when someone has received attunements in higher realms. Once again, your energetic nervous system will be rebooted, imprinted. Your vibration will be raised to higher levels of consciousness. This may take several weeks to integrate into your physical, emotional, mental, and spiritual bodies. You may experience a detoxing during this time. The more you draw the symbols into your hands and chakras, the more you are reinforcing and strengthening your connection with them and the Divine Source that empowers them. They will grow in vibration and healing abilities as you work with them daily. Remember, you are the connection and the channel for this Divine energy to flow through. No ego, no will is involved. The symbols enhance the consciousness of the healing energy from highest Source. They assist the receiver to embrace the healing energy for their highest good, whatever their Spirit needs.

Each symbol is a specific tool, key, vibration and changes or amplifies the Reiki energy as it blends its specific vibration with the Reiki energy, amplifying the healing intention. They can be used individually or together. All are important and offer unlimited healing energy. Never minimize their power to create a healing situation. Visualizing, energetically drawing them into your palms and chakras, drawing them over the recipient, speaking their names, tapping, blowing, and weaving are just a few ways to enhance their energy. Allowing more energy to flow through your crown, from Divine Source, through your heart and hands can create miracles, as long as the recipient's Spirit truly wants one. Healing can take place on many levels. Setting the intention for the recipient's highest good, holding sacred space for the energy, enhanced by the symbols, allows the energy to flow effortlessly and powerfully.

Remember, Reiki can cause no harm and the recipient cannot overdose on the energy. No ego or will is involved in a Reiki session. Empowering the energy with the symbols is a benefit and great gift as they directly connect to Divine Source, Spiritual consciousness.

SYMBOLS DESCRIPTION

Learning the names and how to draw the three Level 2 Reiki symbols will take your practice to new levels of heightened consciousness and effectiveness. The symbols speak and connect you directly to Spiritual consciousness. The three symbols are tools, keys to amplify the Reiki energy you stream from Divine connection. The symbols are ancient. Yes, some are Japanese kanjis, but the energy and meanings attached are ancient. There are said to be up to 300 Reiki symbols written in ancient Tibetan and Buddhist texts. No, Reiki is not a religious practice. Yes, Reiki is Spiritually guided healing energy. Ancient healing symbols were gifts and common practice in ancient times. They are sacred symbols. The respect and gratitude given to the symbols continues to empower them. Only because of the demands and needs of these current times, some of these powerful healing symbols have come to public view and use. Many more will be revealed as the human consciousness progresses. Previously, these symbols were not available to the masses. They were and are still used by trained healers to assist others on their healing journey. It is possible for someone not trained or ready to receive the energy of the symbols to begin an energetic healing process just by looking at the symbols. Without guidance, this can be a disturbing, confusing experience. For this reason, the symbols are kept out of public view.

For many years in modern times, the symbols were not allowed to be written down in class but had to be memorized. Because of this, there are many variations to the way some of the symbols are drawn. The symbols will still carry the intention of the energy they are used for, no matter what variation you learn. It is important for you to draw the symbols exactly the way your master teacher presents them, as this is exactly how they are infused into your energetic system. Each symbol carries a specific energy and vibration. Each symbol is a different tool, a key to access very specific healing vibrations.

The energy and power of these sacred symbols are transferred to another by physical touch and initiation from a master teacher, who has also received their training and initiation from a master teacher. One can read and study all of the books written about Reiki, but the actual passing of the symbols into one's energetic system can only happen through a master teacher.

Daily practice, intention, connection to Divine source, grounding and balancing one's individual energy with the breath and meditation, allows your vibration to be ready to accept these powerful tools. Working with the symbols will continue to unfold your gifts and talents beyond anything you have experienced or imagined. Your energetic system will be re-booted, amplified. You will vibrate and operate at a higher level of consciousness and awareness than ever before!

Activating your Reiki symbols daily will allow your connection to their vibration and consciousness to grow. Energetically drawing and tapping them into the palms of your hands and into your chakras will continue this growth and connection. Repeating their names as you draw them makes them more powerful. Visualize them in your mind constantly. They may appear as brilliant white light or in color. Just thinking about the symbols allows their energy to flow. Use these tools to assist and amplify intentions of highest good.

The Power Symbol

Your first symbol is the "Power Symbol." With many meanings and interpretations in many languages and spiritual or religious practices, the symbol empowers the intention to which it is attached. In Reiki, the Power Symbol increases the strength of the Reiki energy. The Reiki flowing through you becomes supercharged, amplified. Use the Power Symbol to clear and set positive energy in your space and to begin and finish a Reiki session. Use it to pass blessings and love as you touch someone, enhance protection at work, at home, in traffic, enhance affirmations, and in so many other ways. See, hear, and feel the symbol in your mind. Feel the vibration running through every cell of your body.

Several years ago, a dear friend in her late 40s called me, very upset. She had been having some mild health issues. After going to the doctor, they proceeded to order a series of heart tests. The tests showed a blockage in one of her arteries and she was informed that she needed surgery. This information did not feel true to her and she was very upset. As we discussed what the doctor had recommended and also her belief in holistic and alternative medicine, we came up with a plan. Being Reiki trained, she was very open to my suggestion. Since she lived halfway across the country from me, with several time zones difference, we set a time for me to call in the evening. Before our evening call, her homework was to look up and study a picture of the heart and circulatory system of the body. This allowed her to have a clear picture in her mind of a healthy, operating system.

My friend was comfortably in her bed, as we had planned, when I called. Guiding her into a balancing, calming meditation, activating her symbols and slowing, deepening her breathing, we began. In my mind, I was holding her feet, running massive amounts of divine healing Reiki light into her body. We were both seeing the light run through her veins, arteries, and heart, amplified by microscopic Cho Ku Rei symbols. This session continued until I felt her fall asleep. Sealing the work with Cho Ku Rei, that it might continue to flow and clear any obstructions in her circulatory system.

Daily, she continued visualizing the light with the power symbol running through her body. After returning to the doctor the following week and rerunning the medical test, everything was clear and no surgery was needed.

A friend and Reiki student had a high pressure job. Because she had done this work for many years, she was familiar with all of her co-worker's jobs. She had a hard time saying "NO" and setting boundaries at work. Whenever a co-worker had a question or got stuck, they ran into her cubicle, interrupting her own heavy work load, to have her find the answers. As a result, she rarely finished her day on time. She started putting the power symbol, like a woven curtain, over her doorway. Now, others knock, ask for help when she has time, or just figure it out themselves. One Monday morning, she forgot to do her blessing and Reiki her doorway. A very dominating co-worker marched right in, sat on my friend's desk and her work, and began to rant about a problem. My friend looked up with surprise and thought, "Yikes! I forgot to use the Reiki symbol!" She quickly drew the symbol, tiny and unseen, and the other woman jumped up and walked briskly out, in mid sentence! The Reiki caused no harm, just set the dome of protection from unwanted energy.

The Emotional/Mental Symbol

This symbol can be used to heal or enhance any emotion. It balances the right and left hemisphere of the brain. Balancing Yin and Yang, compassion and strength, heart and logic, can be a daily or moment to moment journey. This symbol can enhance and bring ease to this feat. The Emotional/ Mental Symbol can assist in creating new patterns of behavior. It can assist in the healing of addictions (and there are many forms of addictions) and unwanted habits (patterns of behavior).

The symbol can be effective in calming and focusing those who suffer from ADD, ADHD, memory loss, stress, self-esteem, and so much more. See and hear the symbol in your mind. Feel its vibration flowing through every cell of your body.

A new client called, seeking a Reiki session before her upcoming surgery. She was very fearful, so much so that she was unable to function in her normal, daily activities. Her family was becoming afraid that she would not survive the surgery. The client and her life partner came together for a Reiki session. Teaching them both the calming breath was the first exercise. I energetically infused the Emotional/Mental Symbol into them both, all their chakras, while they continued the breath. They were both now calm enough to receive a full session. Weaving the Emotional and Power Symbols into the area of dis-ease, then into her power center, gave her the courage and strength to face the surgery successfully. Her recovery was quick and she contributes this to the Reiki work. She still practices the calming breath.

Another client had a young son with behavioral issues at school; he had actually been expelled from several. She used the Emotional/Mental Symbol on the "mouth of Spirit" spot at the base of his skull nightly. This brought him calmness and focus and he was no longer a distraction or hindrance in class. Upon reaching junior high school, he became a summer camp counselor and worked with other children as a positive role model!

The Distant Healing Symbol

This symbol is composed of Japanese kanji characters. The Japanese interpretation of this symbol is "the origin of all is pure consciousness." What this means is there is no beginning, no end. Past, present, and future exist simultaneously. It is a ladder or doorway to other dimensions. It is a most powerful healing tool. During any Reiki session, this symbol assists in finding the energetic root of the issue causing the dis-comfort or dis-ease. This root can go from the current moment, finding trauma, all the way back to the womb, or to previous lives, or through genetic inheritance. This energy can also be from living in the future and not in the moment. The current collective consciousness can be affecting those who are empathic, highly sensitive, in a negative manner. The Distance Symbol can be used to send Reiki to any intention, being, element, part of our world, cosmos. See and hear the symbol in your mind. Feel the vibration flowing through every cell of your body.

I have a friend who travels a lot for her work, which can be very stressful. As she is Level 2 Reiki trained, she sends the Distant Symbol with calming intentions, weeks ahead of traveling. She sends it to the plane, that it may be on time in a smooth flight, and she sends it to the conference room where she will be facilitating the meeting. The calming energy is already in place for the meeting. Her stress level and insomnia have decreased greatly with this practice.

A family member living many states away called in a state of great physical discomfort and pain. I had her lay on her couch, talked her through the calming breath, and had her hang up the phone. I continued to send her Reiki for 15 minutes. Later that day, we spoke again and I asked her how she felt from receiving the Reiki. She told me she felt a warm bubble of light hold her and comfort her. Her pain dissolved and she was able to sleep, something she had been unable to do peacefully for days.

Realizing that my own issues stemmed from being an unwanted pregnancy, I used the Distant Symbol on myself. Before going to bed, I set the intention to go back to the womb and heal the vibration of feeling unwanted. This was an amazing experience that I still see vividly. I awoke from the experience with so much love, compassion, and understanding of what actually occurred while in my mother's womb. The experience changed my life. I teach this technique in Reiki Master Level training.

CHO KU REI
POWER SYMBOL

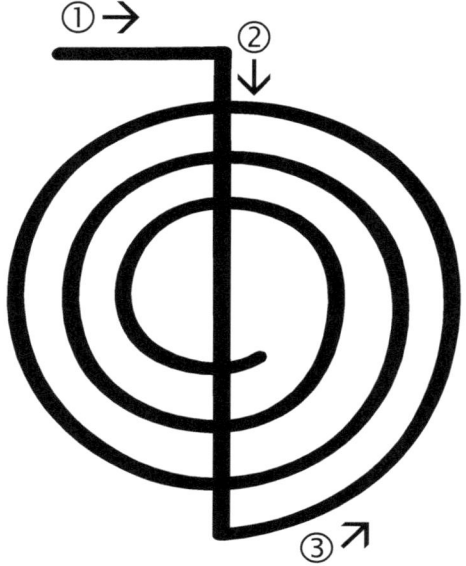

The first symbol you receive in your palms during your Level 1 attunement is the Power Symbol, Cho Ku Rei. It means by "Divine decree," or coming from "Divine Source." Cho Ku Rei empowers, strengthens the Reiki energy by unlimited measure.

Place your hands over the drawing of Cho Ku Rei. Close your eyes. Take a few long deep breaths. Focus on the energy or vibration that begins to emanate from the symbol. Relax, breathe, and allow this vibration to flow through your body. Every symbol has its own unique vibration and use. Now open your eyes, trace the symbol with your fingers. What sensation do you experience? How old does this symbol feel? Remember to trace the symbol exactly as it is drawn, as this is how it is infused into your energetic system.

Cho Ku Rei can be used at the beginning, during, or at the end of any Reiki session. Using Cho Ku Rei at the beginning of a Reiki session will automatically take the vibration of the entire session to greater levels of healing. The symbol can be used throughout the session to direct, empower, and assist in releasing energetic blockages throughout the physical, emotional, mental, and spiritual bodies and any or all chakras and the layers of the auric field. As the releasing is being experienced, Cho Ku Rei is enhancing the volume of vibrational light flowing directly from Divine Source, to fill the space that has been created. We use Cho Ku Rei to seal the Reiki energy into all of the bodies, chakras, and layers of the auric field of the recipient at the end of every session.

When clearing or cleansing a space or object, use Cho Ku Rei. The energy of your intention with any of these actions is greatly amplified. With your hands in Gassho, seeing and feeling Cho Ku Rei in your palms, heart, and crown chakra, ask for the Reiki energy to flow through you to clear and dissolve negative, shadow, or unwanted energies from any space or object. To cleanse a space, hold your hands at heart level, palms facing outward towards the space needing to be cleared. This can be an exterior or interior area. Methodically move your hands as one, as if painting the entire space. If you are cleansing a small object, hold it. Chant out loud, "All negative and unwanted, uninvited energies must leave." Repeat a minimum of three times for past, present and future. We may not know what dimension or time, where or when the energy is from, or how long it has been present. You can ask assistance from your Highest Light Guide and Reiki Guide to assist in this process. You can also ask for the energy's guide to assist it into returning to the Source that it relates or belongs to. As you feel the Reiki flowing, visualize pure love and light filling the area or object. Seal the area by closing the energetic field with Cho Ku Rei. Opening your arms wide, envisioning a white light bubble encasing the area, and say your blessing. Slowly bring your hands together in the motion and intention of sealing Reiki into the energetic bubble. Bring your hands back to your third eye, bowing in gratitude. Step back and cut across your body and through the palms of your hands three times.

Using the above technique of clearing, cleansing, and blessing, is important to create your own Sacred Space. Keeping your home or workspace clear of unwanted psychic energy is important. Daily activation and intention will continue to charge up the protective Reiki light energy and continue to fill your space with Divine, unconditional, unlimited love.

Cho Ku Rei can be used in charging or programming crystals. Crystals, especially clear quartz, can be valuable tools when filled with an intention and charged with Cho Ku Rei. Crystals are generators, computers, and will keep their programming until changed. You can clear the programming by blowing Cho Ku Rei over and around the crystal to clear or cleanse it. Dark crystals such as obsidian, black tourmaline, smokey quartz, or hematite, used for clearing and protection, can be cleared the same way. A charged crystal can enhance the healing intention and the Reiki energy by multiples of thousands of times! The size of the crystal does not matter, they are all powerful. If you choose to use crystals in your Reiki practice, your work can be greatly amplified!

Blessings of any kind, for any purpose, can be filled with greater love and compassion using Cho Ku Rei. If you keep your Reiki energy activated all the time and your symbols charged, you can affect everything and everyone you touch or come in contact with in a positive, loving manner. Energetically, you will radiate a higher vibration of love. Do not minimize the power or the volume of Divine light vibrational energy that can flow through you. Cho Ku Rei is a great key to increase your ability to receive and flow greater volumes of Divine light energy as you adjust and grow with daily practice and activation.

When I first started using the symbols, I drew, tapped, said their names, and strengthened their activation throughout the day. Everything I touched was super charged with Reiki. The interior plants I took care of in commercial office buildings began to flourish even more beautifully. Clients at those accounts began to ask me more often to "place my hands on them" for headaches, neck pain, shoulder pain, back pain, etc., from sitting at their desks for so long. I would quickly draw, see, blow Cho Ku Rei into their area of discomfort. Relief was felt in minutes! They were also encouraged to set a timer on their computers for every thirty minutes, to sit back, take five long deep breaths, roll their shoulders, and drink water. I would place them in a dome of Cho Ku Rei Reiki light as I departed. All of these actions took maybe five minutes of my time. They continued to feel the energy and worked more relaxed and pain free. These same clients began scheduling full Reiki sessions after work.

Several years ago, I received a phone call from one of my mentors, asking a favor. Now, favors are not frequently asked for, especially by this person. Her godchild was getting married. She felt she could not perform the wedding, as the couple to be wed was raised with totally different belief systems around religion, spirituality and healing. Their love was stronger than their programmed upbringing. With my Southern Baptist religious background, and the fact that I look like the girl next door, my mentor believed I was the only one who could blend the two groups together lovingly.

I drove three hours to meet the young couple at the place in Nature they had chosen to perform their sacred union. After discussing their beliefs and ideas about their ceremony, we set a protective, sacred circle of love and light around the perimeter of the property. I built a dome of light up and over the trees, encasing the entire area with light and Cho Ku Rei infused energy. This was sealed with the intention: "Let no one enter this area on their special day who does not carry true love and blessings for their union."

Upon my return home, I charged a crystal with Cho Ku Rei and their intention and put it on my grid. The energy radiated over the next two weeks, until the day of the wedding. The special day arrived. As I parked my car and began walking towards the area, I began to overhear stories. So and so had car trouble and couldn't come, someone else missed their flight, someone else had last minute family or business issues, and so it went on. The people who were present were the ones who truly brought well wishes and love to the ceremony. Judgement and negative feelings stayed away. A beautiful ceremony and a joyful time was had by all who attended!

Students who have faithfully charged their doorways at work and home have been able to prevent abusive co-workers, friends, family members, and unwanted Spirit entities from entering their space. No harm is being done to anyone. The intention of using Reiki, amplified with Cho Ku Rei, creates a higher vibration of Love and Light that the lower vibration of anger, bullying, and abuse cannot enter, or feels so uncomfortable that they do not stay. These people and actions eventually fade away. Only when re-invited does this energy re-enter.

My dogs and cats all lived to be 16, 17, 18, and 22 years old comfortably. They loved the Reiki energy. Infusing them in a dome of Cho Ku Rei Reiki energy daily kept them healthy and vet-visit free. Many students have come to take Reiki classes to benefit their aging, rescued, or ailing pets of all sizes and species.

SEI HEKI
MENTAL/EMOTIONAL SYMBOL

Sei Heki works with the energy of the mental/ emotional bodies and the auric field.

This symbol can balance the right and left hemispheres of the brain, bringing balance, peace, and harmony. Sei Heki can be used to change old patterns of behavior, heal addictions, anxiety, distress, grief, fear, etc. The uses for this symbol are unlimited, as the mental/emotional bodies carry so much information from the past, present, and future.

Place your hands over the drawing of Sei Heki. Close your eyes. Take a few long deep breaths. Focus on the energy or vibration that begins to emanate from the symbol. Relax, breathe, and allow this vibration to flow through your body. Every symbol has its own unique vibration and use. Now open your eyes, trace the symbol with your fingers. What sensation do you experience? How old does this symbol feel? Remember to trace the symbol exactly as it is drawn, as this is how it is infused into your energetic system.

Sei Heki can be used during any Reiki session, at any time. We draw the symbol over the full length of the recipient's torso, at the beginning of every session, along with Cho Ku Rei. Many issues of dis-comfort and dis-ease stem from an emotional or mental origin. As memories of trauma begin to surface, Sei Heki can assist in holding the emotions released around the trauma in pure compassion. Healing can then be experienced in a safe, light-filled, and judgement-free space. This ancient symbol can vibrate to the deepest core of congested/blocked energy, no matter how old, new, or future-projected the congestion/blockage may be.

Sei Heki can assist in identifying the initial area of congestion. This can be found in a chakra or several chakras, and layers of the auric field. As the blocked energy is released in one area, it may journey or travel to another chakra or layer of the auric field. It may jump around and flow through any organ or bodily system. Sei Heki can continue to assist in following the movement and fill with the healing vibration as it moves.

Unwanted habits, or patterns of behavior, as we refer to them, can be removed and reprogrammed with Sei Heki. Addictions of any nature, fears, stress, anxiety, low self esteem, relationships, grief, and many other actions and thoughts that no longer serve the highest good of the health of our physical, emotional, mental, or spiritual bodies can be released. This can be done in a variety of ways.

Write the pattern you wish to change on a piece of paper. Energetically draw Sei Heki over the words. Hold the paper in your hands and infuse it with Reiki energy. Visualize in your mind's eye the pattern melting away now. On another piece of paper write the new pattern you wish to bring in to replace the old energy. Energetically draw Sei Heki over the words. Hold the paper in your hands and infuse it with Reiki energy. Visualize in your mind's eye the new pattern being true now, in the moment. Place both papers on your altar, sacred space, or in your pocket. Charge them as many times a day as the old pattern shows up. Your intention and the Sei Heki-infused Reiki energy will assist you in reprogramming your mental and emotional bodies and auric field.

It takes 40 consecutive days of doing this to establish the new pattern of behavior. You will no longer vibrate the old pattern. If you miss a day, the count to 40 starts over!!!

By wrapping your written words, as discussed above, around a clear quartz crystal, you can greatly amplify the healing intention. Hold the paper-wrapped crystal in your hand and infuse it with Sei Heki Reiki energy. You have now programmed the crystal to send this energy 24/7 to your affirmations! The crystal will continue to send this powerful energy for your specific intention until you clear and reprogram the crystal.

Affirmations, whether written or just verbalized, can be enhanced while infusing the energy with Sei Heki. The power of daily affirmations has been shown by the story of Louise Hay and works for anyone who diligently follows the practice. Affirmations, like the Reiki energy, only work for an individual's highest good of physical, emotional, mental, and spiritual bodies. The power of words has been shown by Masuro Emoto to change and influence water. Since we are 80% water, the power of words can change every cell in our body to health and balance. Words infused with the Sei Heki Reiki energy, coming from pure intention, from our Heart, can assist in creating our own healing miracles, whatever that may be for each of us.

Infusing your home, workspace, or any area in Nature that has received trauma with Sei Heki Reiki energy will assist in healing and bring peace and harmony. This energy can assist the Spirit of those who have lost their physical bodies to move forward into higher realms with peace. Natural passing over, disasters, accidents, all can be brought comfort with Sei Heki. Holding this energy in group traumatic situations can be very effective. Close your eyes, visualize the group or area being held in a huge dome of Divine Light filled with Sei Heki infused Reiki. Hold the vision. Write it down. Infuse the intention in a crystal. Infuse with daily compassion from your heart. The energy is enormous and effective.

Animals can be emotionally affected by chaotic energy in the collective human consciousness, their group species consciousness, and natural disasters. Pets tap into that energy too but also absorb emotional/mental trauma vibrations from their owners.

Sei Heki-infused Reiki energy is extremely effective in all of these instances. The energy is received more gently, bringing calm, as you send the energy from your heart, through your mind's eye. Remember, animals connect through thoughts, telepathy first, then if possible, by touch. As with some people, several treatments may be necessary, according to the amount of trauma that has been received. Love, Love, Love is the key here.

Many years ago, on my early morning walk in the country, I heard a crying in the distance. Finally locating the source, I ran across a field, sending Sei Heki Reiki ahead of me, to a five month old puppy. She was hanging by her back leg that was caught in twisted barbed wire fencing. She was suspended above the ground. I was shocked that the coyotes had not gotten to her. She was very weak, trembling, in shock, apparently had been there for hours. I trusted she would allow me to set her free, as I sent pure love into her heart chakra before I reached her. She could not walk and was totally disoriented. Letting her rest in my lap on the ground, I bathed her in Sei Heki Reiki energy. Feeling the time was right, I put her against my chest, her head on my shoulder, and carried her home. I spoke love to her the entire way. We went directly to the vet clinic. She had the bad cut on her leg cleaned and sutured. It was her only trip to the vet besides shots and neutering in her 16 years of living. She was a most loving companion and I miss her.

A client in my Yoga class lost her husband unexpectedly in an unusual accident. She was in shock, as they were both young when they married and were just now in their mid 30s. As soon as she contacted me, I sent a dome of Sei Heki Reiki, overlaid with Cho Ku Rei, to her and their two young children. The shock and the grief would take some time to heal, but the wave of calming Love helped her and the children through the first several weeks and months afterwards.

A client was sent to me by a mutual friend, to calm her fears before surgery. A brain tumor was found lodged above her left ear. She was literally frightened beyond calming, or so she felt. The surgery would be somewhat tricky and could result in hearing loss and possibly affect other nerves. Her partner was equally nervous and upset. They both came for Reiki sessions together. I literally blanketed them both in cocoons of Sei Heki, overlaid with Cho Ku Rei, to even be able to discuss the surgery. Along with long deep breathing, they both calmed enough to have conversation. We had three sessions before the surgery took place. Everyone was calm, optimistic, and ready when the surgery date arrived. The client was held 24/7 in a bubble of Reiki healing light before, during, and after the procedure. All went well and her life resumed without disability.

HON SHA ZE SHO NEN
LONG DISTANCE SYMBOL

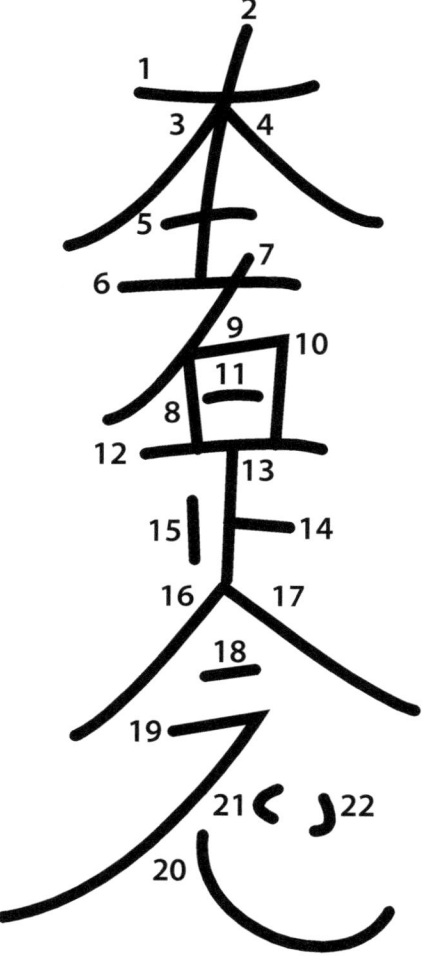

Hon Sha Ze Sho Nen is the long distance symbol. It is a Japanese *Kanji* that has many strokes and meanings. This symbol crosses and bridges all time, space, and all dimensions. Some translations include, "the origin of all is pure consciousness," or "there is no past, no present, no future," or "there is no space or time." Humans are the only species that follow linear time. The Animal, Spirit, and multi dimensional Beings do not operate this way. All is pure consciousness. All time, space, dimensions, and everything, anywhere in creation, past, present, and future are connected in this moment.

Place your hands over the drawing of Hon Sha Ze Sho Nen. Close your eyes. Take a few long deep breaths. Focus on the energy or vibration that begins to emanate from the symbol. Relax, breathe, and allow this vibration to flow through your body. Every symbol has its own unique vibration and use. Now open your eyes, trace the symbol with your fingers. What sensation do you experience? How old does this symbol feel? Remember to trace the symbol exactly as it is drawn, as this is how it is infused into your energetic system.

Hon Sha Ze Sho Nen can be used with every Reiki session, for self and others. Most trauma and fears actually cover the full time-span spectrum. It is believed by many indigenous groups that as we heal, we heal for the past seven generations, current generation, and future seven generations. Using this symbol can enhance and go beyond this belief, healing generations and collective consciousness for all time!

The origin of the trauma could be genetically handed down for generations, karmically brought forward lifetime after lifetime, a product of future fears, ideas, and emotions projected onto us by others or picked up as a psychic attachment, as a few examples. This symbol greatly enhances healing when used in combination with the other symbols. Drawing all the symbols energetically over the recipient at the beginning of a session can allow their combined healing vibrations to work stronger for a more powerful outcome. The highest good of the recipient will be the result.

Hon Sha Ze Sho Nen can assist in healing past trauma, no matter how old, in this and past lifetimes. We can use this symbol to take us back to heal trauma experienced in the womb and at birth. With this symbol, we can go back through previous lifetimes and not only heal trauma but do soul retrieval. At the moment of a traumatic physical death, a soul can fracture, leave a splinter of itself attached to that moment, that space in time. Hon Sha Ze Sho Nen can assist in retrieving and reuniting this splinter to current existence, making a soul whole. This can allow the recipient to move forward in current time with fullness and new energy.

Hon Sha Ze Sho Nen can assist in healing the future. Projected fears of future events can be addressed, infused with Sei Heki, powered with Cho Ku Rei, and overlaid with Hon Sha Ze Sho Nen to calm, release, and heal projections.

The symbol can be sent to a future intention to bring peace, calmness, communication, safety, etc. The symbol sent ahead will infuse and build Reiki light energy for a birth delivery, an important meeting, a long journey, manifesting a project or a relationship. The intentions are unlimited. Sending positive intentions daily, infused with Hon Sha Ze Sho Nen to a future event, creates a super-charged energy bubble to assist and support the intention.

Reiki infused with Hon Sha Ze Sho Nen can be sent to other places, across town, across the country, anywhere on Earth, our galaxy, Creation, or other dimensions. We will practice several techniques to send long distance in this class.

Hon Sha Ze Sho Nen is beneficial to use when removing psychic attachments. We do not know what time, past, present, or future, or what dimension or origin the attached energy/entity has come from. This symbol is very important in assisting the energy/entity to return to its Source.

Charging crystals with Hon Sha Ze Sho Nen empowers the healing intention you are programming. Manifesting goals, changing patterns of behavior, healing for past, present, and future, calming fears, and so much more become super-charged!

A friend of mine became infatuated with our local First Nations history. He read everything he could find in old newspaper articles and books. I noticed a change in his energy. He became more and more depressed, heartbroken. I could sense and feel a strong energetic attachment on him. After explaining to him what a psychic attachment was, he was ready to release it back to its Source. Making the space sacred and ready for the session, I asked for the highest light guides and guardians and whatever great being, held in highest esteem by the attachment, to be present. Drawing in all of the Reiki symbols over my friend, we began. The air in the room changed. The veil between realms became thin, light filling and swirling. Holding my hands wide, Reiki energy filling his auric field, his power center began to glow. In my altered vision, I witnessed a most regal Indian Chief, fully dressed in white traditional clothing, including a full white eagle feather headdress appear. He was surrounded in amazing, brilliant white light. He reached into my friend's glowing power center, and gently pulled out a sphere of golden light. The Chief and the sphere faded into even more brilliant light. The room returned to current time and space…my friend rested. The next day, he was back to being his own true self. The infatuation faded, but the love of the First Nations People did not. He learned how to send love and light for the continued healing of their experiences.

A friend, also a Reiki Master, contacted me to send long distance Reiki to her daughter who was extremely nervous about taking the national exam to enter medical school. We each charged a crystal with the daughter's name, date and location of the test. The test was a month away. To take this test, you are fingerprinted and searched upon entry. Cameras are focused on you during the entire test. The test day arrived. The daughter was calm. The facilitators were unable to get fingerprints! She was still allowed to take the test. She finished early and made very high scores!

Hon Sha Ze Sho Nen allowed me to journey back into my mother's womb to heal the fact that I was an unwanted pregnancy. Holding my adult self in the present, I was able to reprogram the negativity that was running through my mother's energetic body and blood. I was consciously, from conception, sending pure Love and continued connection to great Source, from my adult self to my forming embryo. As I grew and developed in the womb, my adult self programmed love, forgiveness, honor, and respect to my mother. I did not accept her negative programming as it flowed through my body. I kept the life-giving nourishments from my mother, needed to continue my physical development. I kept repeating, "I am a child of love, I remember my connection to Divine Source," over and over and over. When she forced my early delivery, it was my adult self that gave the first touch, pure love. This experience has allowed me to assist many others in their traumatic birth experiences by bringing love and forgiveness to even the most extreme circumstances.

When friends, family, and clients call from out of city, state, or country, requesting Reiki, they always feel the energy as it flows over and through them. A young couple, who were unable to travel to my city, were weekly clients during a time of great trauma. We arranged the day and time for their long distance session. I would call, take them into meditation, as they laid on their bed. We would then hang up and begin the session. Their dog and cat would run in and join them. Both partners received the mental/emotional healing needed during the session. As the session ended, the dog and cat could feel the energy cut, and left the room! They were both older animals and greatly benefitted from the session, too.

Empowering future goals, no matter how far in the future, can be greatly enhanced with Hon Sha Ze Sho Nen. Charge a quartz crystal with your intention, infuse it with all the Reiki symbols, and allow the highest good at the right time to manifest!

At the end of every Reiki Circle, all attendants hold hands in a circle. With all the symbols activated, we send healing light from hand to hand to hand. Flowing the Reiki energy through our feet and radiating the energy out of every cell of our bodies, we open our crowns to even greater volumes of light. The empowered Reiki energy flows through the layers of the earth, into the waters, into the air, touching everything in creation on our planet and beyond. The intention is to enhance healing for the highest good of all species in all realms.

EXERCISES FOR SYMBOLS

Each symbol carries a different vibration. With the following exercises, we will explore how each symbol feels to send and receive. This sensation may vary, but the subtleness will carry a signature.

Bring your hands to Gassho, thumbs at your heart. Close your eyes. Breathe in long and deep, silently chanting Cho Ku Rei. Draw the symbol into each hand, tapping three times after drawing, repeating the name silently each time. Draw the symbol into each chakra, tapping three times and repeating the name silently.

Bring your hands back to Gassho. Close your eyes and feel the Cho Ku Rei energy between your hands, flowing up to your crown, back down through your heart chakra, and out your hands. Envision the Cho Ku Rei energy filling your auric field. Relax your arms down to your lap. Feel the energy streaming through your crown, pulsating all around your auric field, throughout your body and down to your feet.

Separate into pairs and face your partner. One of you is the receiver and one of you is the sender. The receiver sits comfortably with hands on thighs, palms up and eyes closed. The sender leans forward, draws Cho Ku Rei slightly above each knee, tapping in three times and silently repeating the name of the symbol. Place your cupped hands lightly on the receiver's knees. Eyes closed, crown chakra open, flow the Cho Ku Rei Reiki energy into your partner's knees. The touch is so light, like a butterfly landing. Do this for a few minutes. Notice any sensation that may be occurring.

The sender disconnects and sits back. Repeat this exercise, trading positions with your partner. Once completed, each student shares the receiving and sending experience with the class.

Sit back and bring your hands to Gassho, thumbs at your heart. Close your eyes. Breathe in long and deep, silently chanting Sei Heki. Draw the symbol into each hand, tapping three times after drawing, repeating the name silently each time. Draw the symbol into each chakra, tapping three times and repeating the name silently.

Bring your hands back to Gassho. Close your eyes and feel the Sei Heki energy between your hands, flowing up to your crown, back down through your heart chakra, and out your hands. Envision the Sei Heki energy filling your auric field. Relax your arms down to your lap. Feel the energy streaming through your crown, pulsating all around your auric field, throughout your body and down to your feet.

Face your partner. One of you is the receiver and one of you is the sender. The receiver sits comfortably with hands on thighs, palms up and eyes closed. The sender leans forward, draws Sei Heki slightly above each knee, tapping in three times and silently repeating the name of the symbol. Place your cupped hands lightly on the receiver's knees. Eyes closed, crown chakra open, flow the Sei Heki Reiki energy into your partner's knees. The touch is so light, like a butterfly landing. Do this for a few minutes. Notice any sensation that may be occurring.

The sender disconnects and sits back. Repeat this exercise, trading positions with your partner. Once completed, each student shares the receiving and sending experience with the class.

Sit back and bring your hands to Gassho, thumbs at your heart. Close your eyes. Breathe in long and deep, silently chanting Hon Sha Ze Sho Nen. Draw the symbol into each hand, tapping three times after drawing, repeating the name silently each time. Draw the symbol into each chakra, tapping three times and repeating the name silently.

Bring your hands back to Gassho. Close your eyes and feel the Hon Sha Ze Sho Nen energy between your hands, flowing up to your crown, back down through your heart chakra, and out your hands. Envision the energy filling your auric field. Relax your arms down to your lap. Feel the energy streaming through your crown, pulsating all around your auric field, throughout your body and down to your feet.

Face your partner. One of you is the receiver and one of you is the sender. The receiver sits comfortably with hands on thighs, palms up and eyes closed. The sender leans forward, draws Hon Sha Ze Sho Nen slightly above each knee, tapping in three times and silently repeating the name of the symbol. Place your cupped hands lightly on the receiver's knees. Eyes closed, crown chakra open, flow the Hon Sha Ze Sho Nen Reiki energy into your partner's knees. The touch is so light, like a butterfly landing. Do this for a few minutes. Notice any sensation that may be occurring.

The sender disconnects and sits back. Repeat this exercise, trading positions with your partner. Once completed, each student shares the receiving and sending experience with the class.

Everyone cuts the energy and returns to their seats. Now we will focus on one student at a time. This student sits comfortably with their palms facing up on their thighs. The rest of the class places their hands, palms cupped and facing outward, at their heart center. The intention is to now flow Reiki energy to the receiver. Do this flow for a few minutes. Go around the room until everyone has had a turn to receive. Once completed, each student shares the receiving and sending experience with the class.

This is a continual flow of light healing energy that can be with you 24/7. This energy will grow daily, as long as you activate your symbols and your Reiki. It will vibrate through and off of your body, affecting everything and everyone around you in a positive manner!

Everyone stand up and do a few aura strengthening exercises, drink water, get some fresh air and walk around.

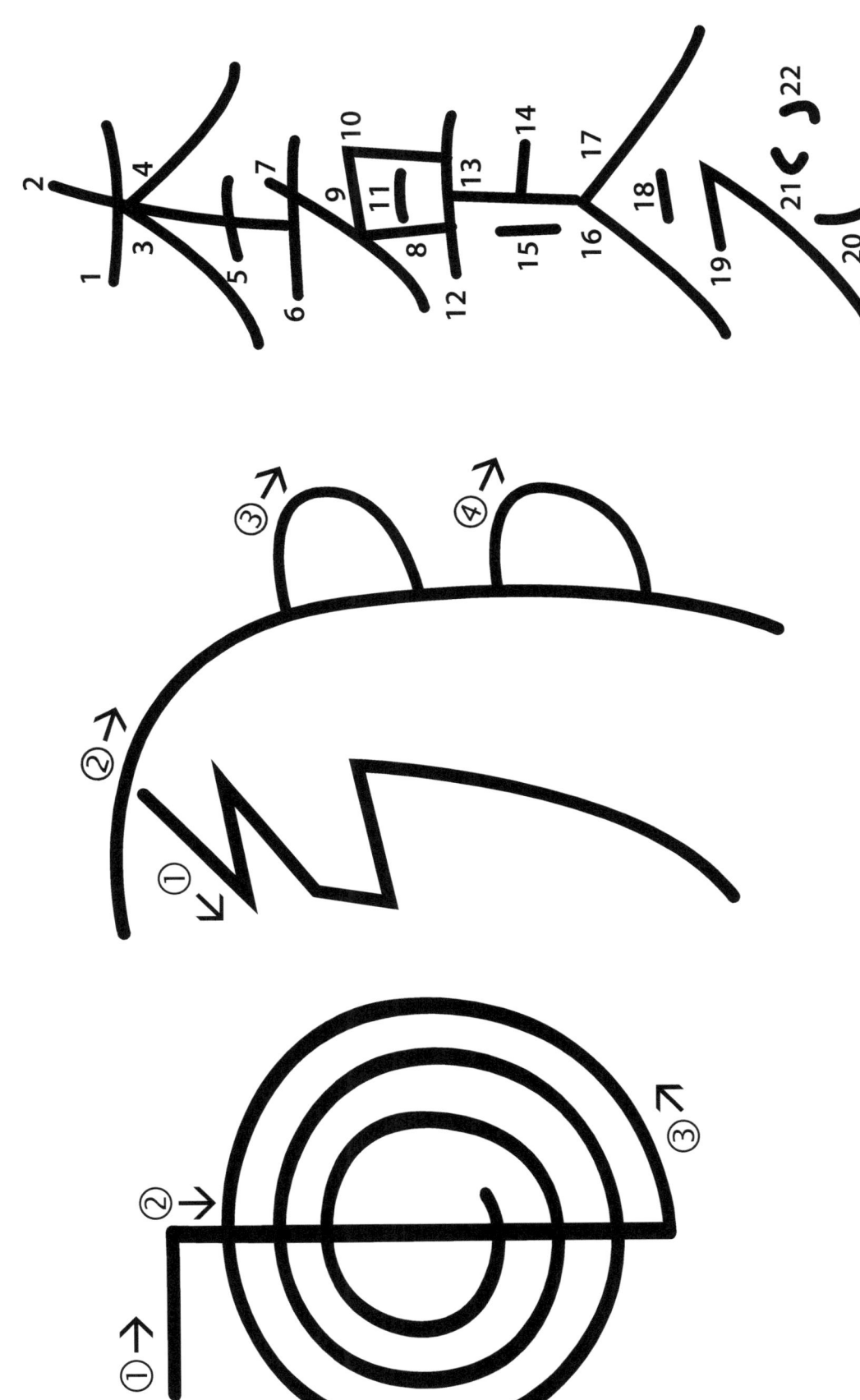

Second Degree Usui Reiki Symbols as drawn by Mrs. Takata

Maha Reiki Level 2 Manual 37

SENDING REIKI WITH THE EYES

Level 2 Reiki is full of multi-tasking! Not only do you have three wonderful symbols as tools, you also have many techniques to increase the flow and direction of the Reiki energy. You will be able to focus on many areas of a recipient at once. Some of these methods were taught by Usui Sensei and some were given to me through Divine Guidance. You will know when to use each method as the moment of need arises. Combinations of symbols and methods increase the amplification and the ability for the Reiki energy to be more powerful. One of the methods is sending Reiki with the eyes.

Usui Sensei taught a method of sending Reiki with the eyes, called *Gyoshi-ho*, meaning "to stare." This method can be used during any session. It can be used when you are called to send Reiki while you are anywhere, in nature, in groups, traffic, etc.

With all of your symbols activated, take a long deep breath, connecting you to your earth chakra and opening your star chakra. Relax your eyes. In your mind's eye, see the symbol you wish to send. Inhale deeply. With highest good intention, as you exhale, send the symbol to the intended area or recipient. Repeat this technique for as long as you are guided to do so. Remember to detach, cut the energy, once you are done.

> **Exercise:** We will go around the group.
> One person at a time will receive the Reiki energy with the eyes.
> Person receiving: breathe several times, long and deep. Relax into your normal breath cycle.
> Practitioners sending Reiki with your eyes, do a quick flow scan of the recipient's energy with your hands.
> Be in the flow. Allow your hands to stop where they want to focus energy.
> Rest your hands in your lap. Relax your eyes.
> Allow the symbol that wants to be present to fill your mind's eye.
> Begin to send this image to the recipient's area where your hands detected the need.
> Stay relaxed. Repeat silently the name of the symbol as you continue to send with your eyes.
> Another area of need or symbol may come into your mind's eye after a short time.
> Allow your eyes to follow the flow.
> If the symbol changes, continue the silent chant, seeing this symbol in your mind's eye.
> When time is completed, detach and cut your energy from the recipient.
> **Discussion:** brief discussion with each sender and receiver. Go to next student.

Sending Reiki with your eyes during a session can allow you to multi-task. Your hands may be at two places or two levels already, but your attention is also being drawn to a third location. Send Reiki with your eyes to this location. Reiki can be sent with your eyes when you witness someone or something in any type of trauma. Asking permission of the Spirit of the person, area, animal, etc., is important to do before sending. You will receive an answer by telepathy or a knowing. Sending Reiki ahead of your car in traffic can be beneficial. The possibilities are unlimited!

SENDING REIKI WITH THE BREATH

Another method of sending Reiki is with your breath. Usui Sensei taught a method of sending Reiki with breath, called *Koki-Ho*. Your breath is a sacred, powerful tool. Your breath is your life-force. Overlaid and protected with Reiki energy, your breath can become a powerful tool to assist others in healing. This method can be used to enhance the Reiki energy during any session, anywhere.

With all of your symbols activated, take a long deep breath connecting you to your earth chakra and opening your star chakra.
Feel your root chakra. See with your mind's eye the symbols resting there.
On the next breath, tighten all of the muscles in the area of your root chakra, anal and vaginal (if female). Feel the tightening of the muscles in this area pulling upward as they contract.
Hold this breath and contraction movement.

We will now refer to this as the *root lock*, or *Hui Yin* point. Now exhale and relax.
The Hui Yin, when contracted, seals and strengthens the flow of life force moving upward.
Now inhale, contract the Hui Yin. Place the tip of your tongue on the roof of your mouth, draw Cho Ku Rei on the roof of your mouth. Keep your tongue placed on the roof of your mouth, just behind your teeth. Exhale, strong and steady, Cho Ku Rei. Keep the Hui Yin contracted as you do this!
Practice this breath several times.

You can feel a difference on the back of your own hands when you are blowing the symbol without the Hui Yin contracted as to when it is contracted.
Repeat for several minutes.
Discuss this exercise with each student in the group.

Once again, breathe in, contract the Hui Yin. Draw Sei Heki on the roof of your mouth.
Keeping your tongue in place on the roof of your mouth and just behind your teeth, exhale
Sei Heki strong and steady, with the Hui Yin still contracted.
Practice this breath several times.

Feel the power and vibration of Sei Heki on the back of your own hands as you practice.
Repeat for several minutes.
Discuss this exercise with each student in the group.

Now, we will activate Hon Sha Ze Sho Nen.
Once again, breathe in, contract the Hui Yin.
Draw Hon Sha Ze Sho Nen on the roof of your mouth.
Keeping your tongue in place on the roof of your mouth and just behind your teeth, exhale
Hon Sha Ze Sho Nen strong and steady, with the Hui Yin still contracted.
Practice this breath several times.

Feel the power and vibration of Hon Sha Ze Sho Nen on the back of your own hands as you practice. Repeat for several minutes.

Discuss this exercise with each student in the group.

Using the breath to amplify the vibration of the symbol can be very beneficial to a recipient.
Drawing the symbols on the roof of your mouth, at the beginning of your day, with the intention that they remain infused, will keep them activated for the moment when you need them.
When giving a Reiki session, you can blow the symbols through the back of your hands to amplify the energy. Your hands can be together, stacked a few inches apart, or in different layers of the auric field. You can cup your hands and blow the symbols through them, directly into a chakra or place of trauma. Blowing three times, past, present, future, is recommended.

Blowing Cho Ku Rei to clear or cleanse an area, object, or crystal can be highly effective.
Filling a room by blowing your Reiki symbols through the back of your hands increases the amplification of their energy. This technique is very beneficial to assist in the calmness, healing of animals and young children, as they are very sensitive. Filling their space with the healing vibration will allow them to absorb the energy more gently. This method also works great in a workplace.

SENDING REIKI LONG DISTANCE

There are several ways to send Reiki energy long distance. All are effective and beneficial to the recipient. Reiki can be sent anywhere, to any time, using the Hon Sha Ze Sho Nen symbol.

Long distance is used when a recipient is unable to travel or lives out of your area. If you do not know the recipient, it is important to know their name, location, age, and condition. An actual picture of the recipient is good. The recipient could be a person, a group, an animal, or a place.

To give an actual session, schedule a specific day and time, just as you would if they were coming to your space. Confirming the appointed time is important. You want the recipient to be comfortable and ready. Call at the appointment time, take them into meditation, then hang up and proceed with the session. Visualize the recipient on your Reiki Table. If you have a picture, put the picture on the pillow of your table. Activate and draw all of your Reiki symbols over the table. Say your Gassho for this being. Be in the flow of the Reiki energy and allow the guidance from highest light guides and guardians to assist in the session. Use all of your methods and symbols as you are guided. Complete the session as you normally would. Seal the energy and give gratitude. Remember to detach, cut the energetic ties, and clear the energy from your table.

Check in with them later, after they have rested, to answer questions or share beneficial information that you or they received during the session.

A teddy bear or other stuffed animal can be used as a substitute for the actual recipient. You can place their name and/or picture on the teddy bear. Say Gassho for this being. Draw the all the Reiki symbols over the bear. Ask for their highest light guides and guardians to be present and assist in this healing for highest good for the recipient. Proceed as you would for a regular session.

For shorter long distance sessions, hold the recipient's picture or name, with their age, location, and condition, in your Reiki-activated hands. Be in a comfortable position. Draw the Reiki symbols over their name, picture. Say Gassho for this being. Ask for their highest light guides and guardians to assist in this healing of their highest good. Proceed with the sending. When finished, seal the energy, give prayer of gratitude, detach, cut and clear the energy.

When sending long distance Reiki to someone or something who does not know you are doing so, ask permission from their Spirit. You will receive a knowing to proceed or not. When sending Reiki to natural disasters or war torn areas, blanket the entire area with the Reiki symbols so the innocent spirits of all species can receive healing.

The human species has poisoned and polluted our Mother Earth in innumerable ways. Send Reiki, infused with the symbols, through the waters of the Earth for the healing of the waters and all her inhabitants. Remember the experiments of Emoto and water! Send Reiki, infused with the symbols, through the Earth herself, for healing from toxins, fracking, dumping, etc. All beings in the Earth will receive the energy. Send Reiki, infused with the symbols, through the air to clean and refresh the atmosphere.

Remember, Hon Sha Ze Sho Nen can send healing Reiki energy through any time or dimension. The possibilities are limitless!

In my very first Level 2 class, we had an amazing experience when sending Reiki long distance. During the actual class, my younger brother was poisoned while spraying landscape pesticides for the hotel he worked for on Kauai. He was given the wrong protective suit for the chemical he was issued to spray. After hours of being coated, basted in this highly toxic chemical, he was rushed to the hospital. My family contacted me immediately. People exposed to even a small percent of this chemical die. My students and I sat on the floor in a small circle, hands facing up, fingertips touching. My brother's name and location was resting in our hands. We activated all the Reiki symbols, said Gassho, and called in highest light guides, guardians, angels, ascended masters, whoever could assist my brother's Spirit in making a decision to stay or go. The energy was immense. After a short time, I saw a glow of light radiating brighter and brighter from our hands. In the middle of the light appeared a newborn baby, fresh, pink, and laughing. As the vision faded, I knew all was well and it was time to close the session. Gratitude, cutting and clearing followed. My family called that evening to report my brother was having a miraculous recovery and would probably be released in a few days. The chemical company and doctors were completely baffled by his recovery. That was ten years ago. My brother has had health issues over this time. But he is alive, functioning, and was gifted a second chance to live his life, as his Spirit so chose. So much gratitude…

WEAVING WITH CHO KU REI

In the Level 1 Maha Reiki® Manual there was a story about a young woman who miraculously recovered from an extremely life threatening situation. During my time with her in the hospital, just hours after she was admitted, Jesus and Mary appeared as her highest light guardians. They removed thousands of attachments from her physical, emotional, mental, and spiritual bodies. All of her major organs were bleeding. I received the information to "weave the power symbol" around each organ at that time. Visualizing the finest thread of brilliant light, I wove a Cho Ku Rei sock around each organ that was bleeding. These light socks remained in place for weeks, charged daily on my Reiki grid, even after she was released from the hospital.

Since that time, the weaving has become a standard practice for recipients who have physical dis-ease and dis-comfort issues. Organs, joints, bones, auric field layers, all can benefit from the weaving. The weaving can be used on any species. Domes of woven light can be placed over and around any location. Placed on a healing grid, the recipient's weaving receives healing Reiki energy 24/7. We can use this technique on ourselves. One student weaves a unitard of Cho Ku Rei, like a Spiderman suit, and puts it on before she gets dressed every day. Her intention is protection from the toxic environment in which she works.

Asking permission from a client to place a woven mesh around their trauma is important. Once you explain what you are doing, it makes sense to them. Then empower your client with a visualization that they have a mesh of light around the area of concern, and have them continue to run light from their connection to Divine Source to keep it illuminated. Also tell them you will keep it activated 24/7 on your healing grid, with their permission.

Amazing results can manifest!

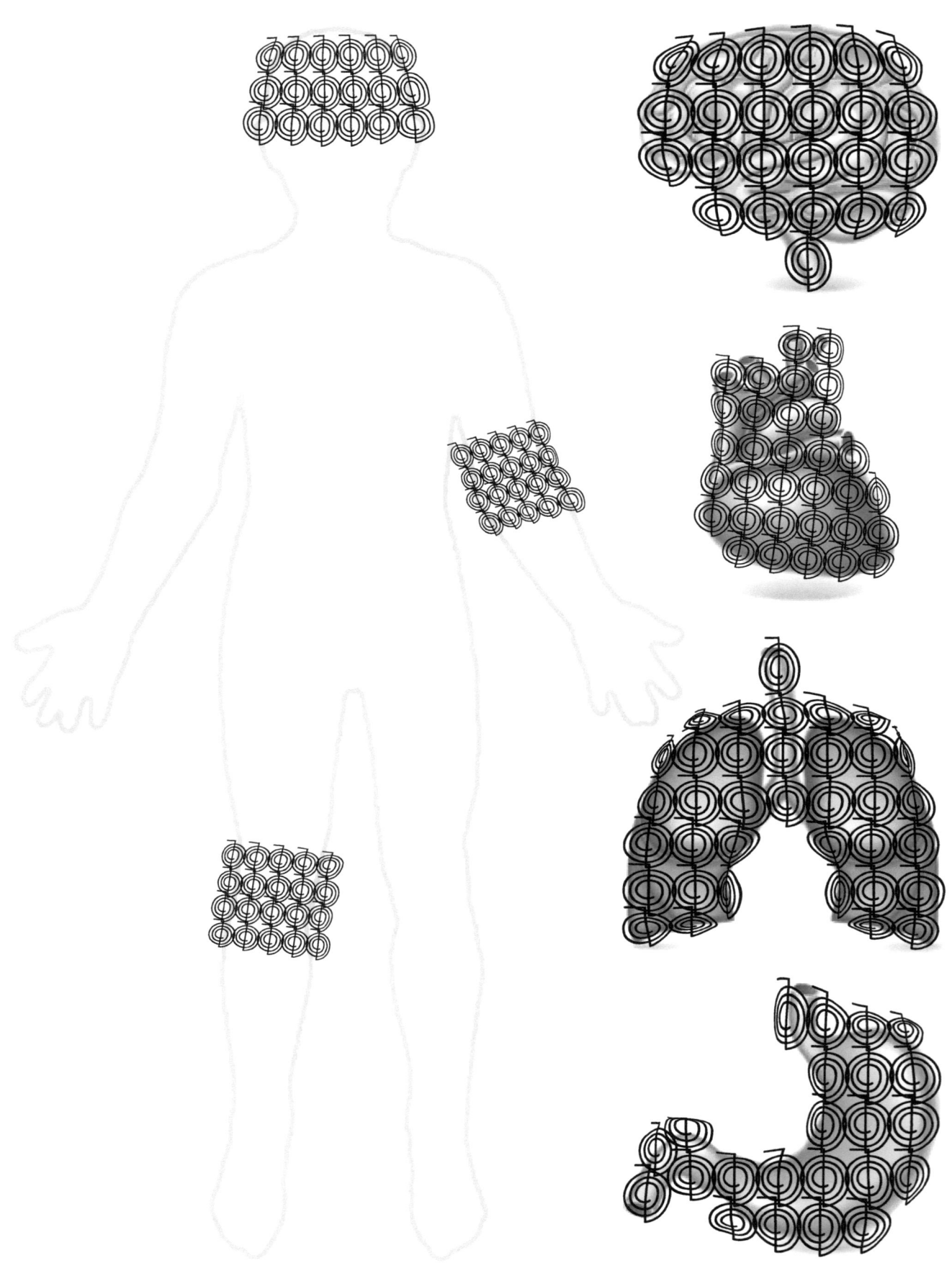

PLANTING STARS AND RUNNING LIGHT

Planting stars is another method of healing that was given to me by Reiki Guides. In a one week period, I saw several clients with kidney and gall stones. Getting to the root of their issues energetically was a key and the focus of their sessions. Once the root is discovered, healing can take place.

During one of the sessions I received the telepathic message: "Plant a star, swallowed from Divine Light, into their organ."

Teaching clients to visualize swallowing or planting a star can take patience. Do not rush this process. Gentle words, compassionate guidance is needed. Once the star is in place, describe it as combusting, spinning white light that is melting away stones and blockages, grain by grain. Clients have been successful with this technique. Surgeries have been cancelled due to the fact the stones no longer showed up on the ultrasound!

Running light through the veins of the body was given to me by Reiki Guides as I worked with clients experiencing catastrophic dis-eases, such as cancer and lupus.

Teaching your clients the long deep breathing exercise, connecting to the Earth and the Heavens, is important at the beginning of every session. This calms and relaxes them. Getting them to visualize is not always easy. If they can close their eyes and remember, feel the full sun shining on them, that is a start. Take it further by having them see/feel the light as the brightest, whitest light, like diving into the center of a white sun.

Have them breathe in this light, feeling it run throughout their body. Next, have them run the light through their veins. Their blood is now glowing with light, creating new light nourishment to every cell in their body. Every cell is now glowing with light and wellness.

Old, dis-eased cells are melting away and fresh, healthy cells are growing, infused with light. Every cell is receiving fresh energy, carried by the light streaming from their connection to Divine Source. This takes daily practice.

Teach them a mantra such as, "I am a child of light," or "Divine Light runs through my blood," to repeat hundreds of times a day. We are beings of light, we have just forgotten!

ANATOMY FOR REIKI - FRONT VIEW

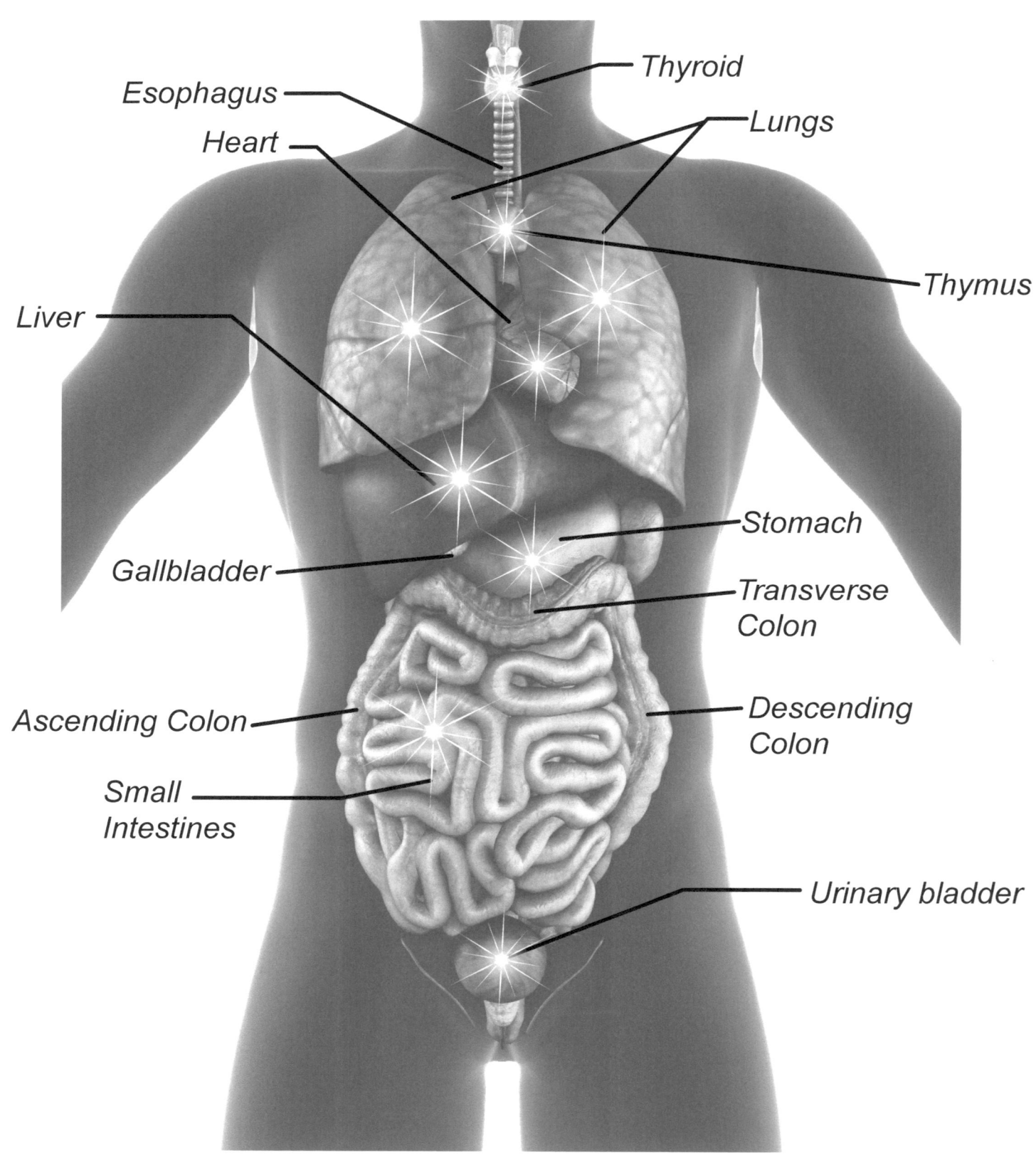

ANATOMY FOR REIKI - BACK VIEW

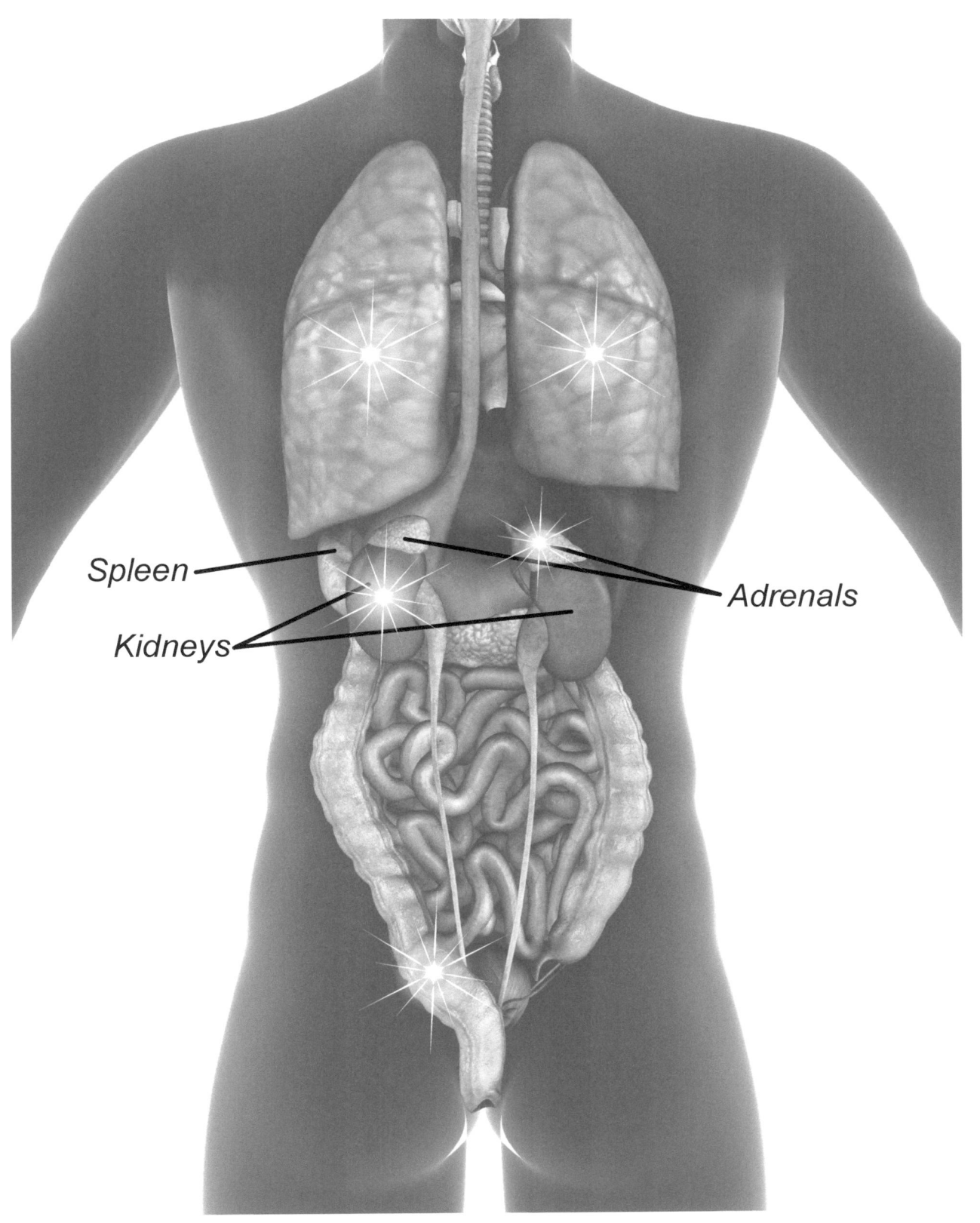

RUNNING LIGHT THROUGH THE HEART AND CIRCULATORY SYSTEM

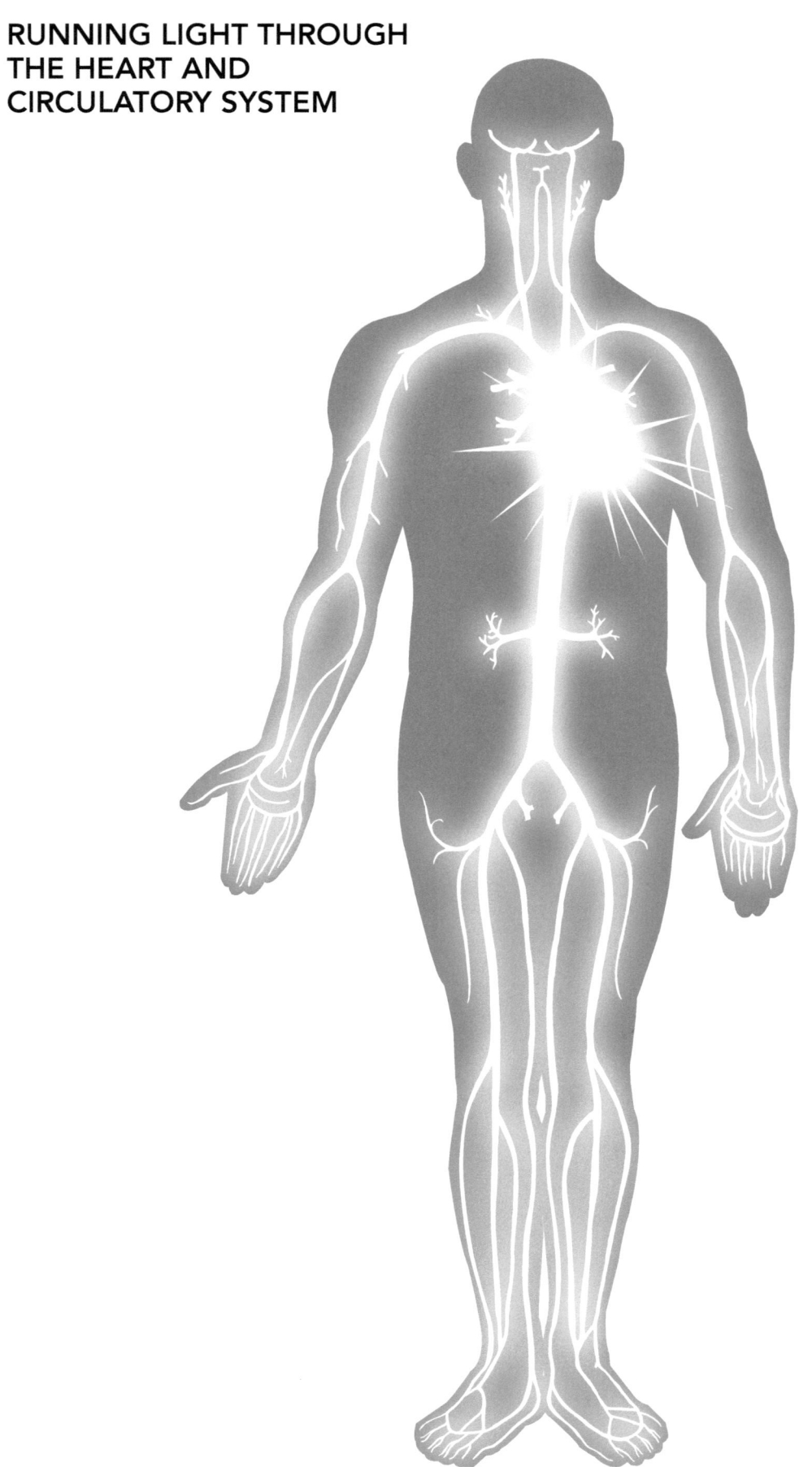

LOUISE HAY

Louise Hay's childhood years were very difficult. She relates that she and her mother were physically abused by her stepfather and that when she was about five she was raped by a neighbor. She dropped out high school at the age of 15.

At the age of 24, she began a modeling career in New York. In 1954, she married Andrew Hay, a successful businessman. After 14 years of marriage, she was devastated when Andrew left her for another woman.

It was during this period she found a church which taught her about the transformative power of thought and that positive thinking could heal the body.

At the age of 51, Hay was diagnosed with incurable cervical cancer. She came to the conclusion that holding on to her anger and resentment of her early childhood traumas had contributed to its onset.

Refusing conventional medical treatment, she began a daily regime of forgiveness, proper nutrition, and reflexology. Louise began by looking in the mirror and saying to herself, "I Love You." She went through every feature and organ, repeating the affirmation. Through the repetition and constant daily reprogramming, Louise convinced herself that she truly loved every cell in her body. She rid herself of the disease and was completely healed.

Louise began writing small, easy to read and to understand books with colorful covers, to assist others in their healing. Embracing self empowerment, love and respect, devoted daily practice of speaking affirmations, healthy diet, eliminating stressful relationships (personal and work), and developing a spiritual practice, were the gifts of her teachings.

Louise Hay went on to become a successful motivational author and founder of Hay House, a publisher of new thought and self-help books. She is responsible for the success of many of the well-known alternative healing authors and teachers who have helped so many people over the past several decades. Hay House has and continues to host world wide teaching and healing seminars.

Louise passed away in 2017 at the age of 91. She leaves a great healing legacy to continue.

While Louise Hay worked with positive affirmations to heal herself, a Japanese individual, Masaru Emoto, experimented with water to show that it could be influenced by words, pictures, and music.

MASARU EMOTO

Masaru Emoto was a Japanese author, researcher, photographer, and entrepreneur, who showed through his experiments with water that human consciousness has an effect on the molecular structure of water.

Emoto experimented with frozen mountain stream water. Water exposed to positive thoughts, affirmations, etc., would produce beautiful crystalline structures when frozen. Conversely, water exposed to negative thoughts, words, etc., would not form crystals.

In one of Emoto's experiments, he took a gallon of fresh spring water, and poured it into several glasses. He taped the following words to the glasses: love, hate, beautiful, ugly, smart, stupid, kill, hug. A group of elementary school children walked by and spoke the words written on each glass. Emoto then took the glasses to his laboratory, a large walk-in freezer.

Once the water was frozen, crystals from each glass were observed under a microscope. All of the positive words created beautiful crystal structures, full of light. The samples from all of the negative words produced malformed blobs of dark colors. Words affect the structural makeup of water.

The human body consists of 70% to 90% water. Every cell in the body contains water. Continual programming with words, music, and pictures affects the water in our cells. Daily affirmations can be a powerful tool for creating wellness in our own bodies. Louise Hay gave us proof of this technique through her personal healing of her cancer.

Taking back personal power and respect, balancing one's energy and health, begins with self-love, forgiveness, and reprogramming every cell of the body. Voicing healing words daily, many times, can create the paradigm of wellness in our physical, emotional, mental, and spiritual bodies.

Masaru Emoto passed in 2014, at the age of 71 years. His work continues on. Many times, during natural disasters, he called on the world peoples to send love through the waters of the Earth to assist in healing. Millions of people continue with this practice.

There are many amazing videos available on his website: *masaru-emoto.net*

MANTRAS

A mantra is a specific formula of sacred words, which by the power of its sound, or vibratory signature, creates specific results in the world of one's body, emotions, mind, and soul. Mantras are ancient, powerful, and they work! The word *mantra* is derived from two Sanskrit words, *manas* or mind, and *trai*, meaning to protect or to free from. Therefore, the word *mantra* means "to free the mind," or "to protect and liberate from delusion."

Sanskrit is the oldest known written language. It is a pure language. Computers can completely break down Sanskrit into mathematics and speak it, just as in sacred geometry.

As you speak Sanskrit, the tip of your tongue touches specific points on the roof of your mouth. The specific words activate the 70,000 nerve points throughout your body. The combination of Sanskrit words forming a mantra works for specific healing issues.

Sound is energy or force. Sound is a spiritual power; it is pure energy which is qualified, shaped, and made manifest within the physical world by our words. Knowing this, one can easily understand how specific sound and word formulas can have a profound influence upon consciousness and the world around us.

The ageless wisdom of the East teaches that the repetition of the syllables of the mantra gradually purifies each of the elements within our body. This is a very important aspect of our transformation, considering that much of our subconscious mind contains the primitive thought-forms and ignorance of the collective consciousness of humanity. The dedicated and consistent use of mantra will refine, purify, and transform this deeply embedded conditioning, which is stored in the organs and glands of the physical body and in the subtle bodies. In this way, we have a tool to make our body/mind a temple of peace, compassion, and wisdom.

Since the beginning of time, shamans, healers, priests, medicine men/women, mystics, and yogis have been aware of the power of specific word or sound formulas, which are either sung, spoken out loud or silently repeated within. All cultures have used words of power for a variety of predetermined purposes. Words of power, or mantras, have been used throughout time as an aid for meditation, healing, protection, and for initiating personal transformation and actually awakening. The sacred syllables (mantras) are prayers for emotional, mental, and spiritual expansion. It is said that the mantra actually carries and bestows the energy of Divinity; the Divine Attributes of specific aspects of God.

The journey from mantra to liberation is a wondrous one. The mantra purifies and expands our consciousness, bringing us into harmony with the very essence of cosmic existence. The sound patterns and thought-forms contained within the sacred syllables of the mantra can align our consciousness with the Consciousness of Light, charging our beings with the powers and rapture of the Divine Mind and Heart.

While there are many very powerful mantras, these are the two we use in Maha Reiki®.

OM MANI PADME HUM MANTRA
(OM MA-NEE PAD-MAY HUM)

Om is a sacred word found in many religions. *Mani* means jewel, *Padme* means lotus flower, and *Hum* is the spirit of enlightenment.

Om
The sound Om is believed to be the primordial sound of all creation. Since the sound Om created the universe, it is believed that it holds within it all that is, was, or will ever be. Om helps to achieve perfection in the practice of generosity.

Ma
This syllable helps in the practice of pure ethics and dissolves jealousy and attachment to fleeting pleasures.

Ni
This syllable helps in achieving perfection in tolerance and patience in ourselves and others.

Pad
This syllable helps dissolve our attachment to prejudices and judgments while helping achieve perfection in perseverance.

Me
This syllable helps in achieving perfection in our powers of concentration and wisdom.

Hum
This syllable helps in dissolving attachments to aggression and hatred. It promotes internal unshakeable and unmovable wisdom.

This mantra means "The jewel of the lotus," or "Praise to the jewel in the lotus."

MEDICINE BUDDHA MANTRA

TAYATA OM BHEKANDZE BHEKANDZE MAHA BHEKANDZE RANDZA SAMUNGATE SOHA

In Tibetan pronunciation, the mantra is as follows:

Tad-ya-ta Om Be-kan-dze Be-kan-dze Ma-ha Be-kan-dze Ra-dza Sa-mung-ga-te So-ha
"Hail! Appear, O Healer, O Healer, O Great Healer, O King of Healing!"

Tayata - means gone beyond
Om - means jewel holder, auspicious one
Bhekandze Bhekandze - means calling Medicine Buddha twice
Maha Bhekandze - means greatness of Medicine Buddha
Randza Samungate - means perfectly liberated or awakened
Soha - means dissolves in me

The Medicine Buddha Mantra can help us to eliminate problems, unhappiness, and suffering. It helps us to gain success, happiness, and promotes inner growth and development.

It is believed that any living being who hears the name of Medicine Buddha never gets reborn in the lower realms - that is the benefit, the power of just hearing the name, the mantra. The reason there is so much power is due to Medicine Buddha's compassion. In the past when he was a bodhisattva, he made so many prayers and dedications with strong compassion in his name, for wishes to be fulfilled and to bring happiness.

CRYSTALS

Quartz crystals have been on Earth since the beginning of time. They have been used by ancient civilizations as protective talismans, peace offerings, and jewelry. We do not know the earliest times that crystals began to be used, but we do know that amulets of Baltic amber have been dated back 30,000 years and British amber beads have been found that are 10,000 years old. Beads from a grave in Russia have dated back 60,000 years.

Records indicate that the ancient Sumerians included crystals in their magic formulas. Ancient Egyptians used crystals and stones for protection, health, and jewelry. The ancient Greeks also used crystals for a variety of purposes. The word *crystal* comes from a Greek word for ice. It was believed that clear quartz was water that was frozen solid.

Throughout history crystals and gemstones have been used by various religions. They are mentioned in both the Bible and the Koran. In Hinduism the Kalpa Tree, an offering to the gods, was said to be made of precious stones. A Buddhist text from the 7th century describes a diamond throne.

In Europe, from the 11th century through the Renaissance, the virtues of precious and semi-precious stones can be found in medical records. During the Age of Enlightenment which came after the Renaissance period, the use of crystals began to fall from favor in Europe. Many tribal cultures around the world continued to use crystals and stones in their healing and spiritual practices. With the New Age culture which began in the 1980s, the use of crystals and gemstones began to re-emerge as a healing alternative method. It is now viewed as more mainstream in today's world.

Crystals hold information from the beginning of the Earth's formation. It is believed by some that ancient wisdom has been programmed into crystals from higher dimensional beings. As the human species is ready to learn and accept this information, these crystals are surfacing. An example of this is the Lumerian quartz crystals. They are said to hold information pertaining to the Akashic records. When used in meditation, information can be revealed to assist in healing, raising consciousness, and unfolding new evolutionary information.

Clear quartz crystals are like mini computers and can be programmed with intention. They will hold the intention and programming until cleared and reset. Computer chips are made from silicon (quartz). Our technological advancement can be attributed to the use and understanding of the qualities of quartz.

We can use crystals to enhance our Reiki practice. The chapter on Chakras in the Level 1 manual discusses crystals that affect each chakra. Black crystals can be used to absorb shadow energy. In a Reiki session, we can program crystals with the Reiki symbols to amplify the Reiki energy for even greater healing abilities. Be sure to clear the crystal after each client and recharge.

Clear quartz crystals are used on the Reiki healing grids. We will discuss this in depth, with the grids.

REIKI HEALING GRIDS

From time infinite, many tools have been used by people all over the world to enhance healing. We find evidence of this in ancient stone carvings in caves, on pyramids, and in ancient writings and paintings. Some of these have taken the form of grids, circles, sacred geometry, medicine wheels, prayer wheels, etc.

We will learn to use a healing grid, enhanced with Reiki-charged crystals and sacred geometry, for the intention of sending Reiki healing energy 24 hours a day, seven days a week! There is no time, distance, or dimensional barrier when using your grid. Pure intention, for the highest good, super-charged with the Reiki symbols and programmed crystals on sacred geometry, is indeed a very powerful computer.

We have chosen to use the seed of the Flower of Life, sacred geometry, as our grid. Two other shapes, the Antahkarana and the MerKaBa are included for your choice, also. You can use as many grids as you feel compelled to use.

For the Flower of Life grid, you will need six small clear quartz crystals, one master clear quartz crystal, and one pyramid or other shaped clear quartz crystal. It is advised to have a nice number of additional small clear quartz crystals, to use for special intentions.

Clear and cleanse all of your crystals before using on your grid. If you have had time to charge them with the sun and moon, good. Clearing can be done with smudging also. Blowing Cho Ku Rei around the crystal with the intention of clearing of energy is also very good.

Hold each crystal in your hand. With all of your Reiki symbols activated, blow each symbol into each crystal. Holding all of the crystals in your hand, fill them with the intention of being your special grid healers to send healing energy for the highest good to all whose names you place on the grid. This can also include personal goals, areas of the world or cosmos, a collective good purpose, etc.

Your crystal grid is now ready to be set up:

> Hold your Reiki charged hands over your grid. Feel the vibration of the Flower of Life.
>
> Infuse the grid with pure love, light, and compassion.
>
> Set your Reiki infused crystals on your grid.
>
> Again place your hands over your grid. Continue to infuse the grid with Reiki.
>
> Raise your hands a little higher. Feel the energy growing?

It will grow daily, as you charge it with intention of pure love, light, and compassion.

Pick up your Master crystal. This will always stay on the corner of the grid.

Hold and super charge the Master crystal with the symbols and intention.

Begin uniting all of the energies of the crystals into one by using the Master crystal.

Start in the center. Follow the first circle you choose, circling back to the center.

As you circle, chant in your mind or out loud, Cho Ku Rei.

Make a complete round of all the circles, chanting Cho Ku Rei.

Repeat this complete grid movement with Sei Heki.

Repeat this complete grid movement with Hon Sha Ze Sho Nen.

Now for your final round, chant something like, "I infuse this grid with pure love, light, and compassion."

Chant from your heart.

Do not minimize the power of the intention you are programming!

FLOWER OF LIFE/SACRED GEOMETRY

The "Flower of Life" can be found in all major religions. This image is thousands of years old and can be found embedded in ancient sacred sites around the world.

The symbol mathematically contains all knowledge, all energy, all conscious thought, and structures that form the building blocks of life. Many say it contains the vibration of the Creator and through this symbol, can communicate directly.

The Flower of Life contains a sacred power which activates energy coding within your mind, assisting you to access higher vibrational presence.

Within this geometric image can be found the Platonic Solids which are mathematically the building blocks of the Universe. They form the basis of all life, language, music, and conscious thought.

ANTAHKARANA

The Antahkarana is a multidimensional ancient healing and meditation symbol. It has been used for thousands of years in China and Tibet. It enhances all energetic work by neutralizing negative energy and creating a positive effect on the chakras and aura.

The origin of the symbol is unknown. Through psychic readings, it is believed that the symbol was brought to earth over 100,000 years ago during the Lemurian times to assist humans with connecting to the higher self. It is thought to be a bridge which connects the higher mind with the other levels of the body.

The symbol is made up of three sevens which represent the seven chakras, the seven colors, and the seven tones of the musical scale.

Since the symbol has its own consciousness, it works to increase all healing. It can never be misused or cause harm.

MERKABA

The general meaning of MerKaBa is chariot, cart, or "thing to ride in." The MerKaBa is a spinning structure of light, much like the chakras. When it is spinning properly, it works as an inter-dimensional gateway so that a person can ascend to higher consciousness.

The MerKaBa is referenced in many spiritual and religious texts. In the Bible there were wheels, the MerKaBa, by which Ezekiel was able to ascend into heaven. The MerKaBa is mentioned in the Torah as the Merkavah. The meanings are Chariot and Throne of God. In Egypt this sacred geometric pattern was known as Mer-Ka-Ba. It was three separate words: *Mer* meant a kind of light that rotated within itself; *Ka* meant spirit, the human spirit; and *Ba* meant the human body. The entire word, *Mer-Ka-Ba*, meant a rotating light that would take spirit and the body from one world into another.

In the Third Dimension, the MerKaBa is a complex Platonic solid, a form of sacred geometry. It is also an electromagnetic field within the microwave range. It is also believed that it is a living field which responds to human thoughts and feelings and connects the human mind and heart.

DAILY PRACTICE

Take five, 10, 15, 20 or more minutes, whatever you can give, to start your day calm and balanced. Remember, it takes 40 days to establish a new pattern of behavior!

Activate your Reiki Symbols

Activate your Reiki upon waking up! I never turn mine off, but ask that it be activated 24/7. However, I believe showing gratitude and saying the name of Reiki adds strength to the energy.

Balance your Chakras with the Chakra meditation.

Aura Strengthening

Start every morning with this exercise, as soon as your feet hit the floor!
Repeat as many times as day as needed. At work, fellow employees think you are just stretching out, so do it without worry. Teach it to your friends at work, too. And don't forget to cut, cut, cut away unwanted energy that you are exposed to.

Recite your affirmations

Usui Sensei gave us the example of the five precepts. You can use these or create your own. Use your voice!

Breath

Breath is sacred. It is our life force that flows through every cell of our body. In many cases, traumatic life experiences and stress, no matter what creates it, has taken our breath away. Taking the time to re-train our breath to be full and rich, takes daily practice. Sometimes, moment to moment practice is needed. For ourselves, doing the chakra meditation every morning, and/or during the day, can help keep us balanced, relieve stress and relieve minor physical discomfort.

To self-empower family, friends and others, teach them!
Take the time to take a very long deep breath, up from the bottoms of the feet, all the way up through the body, reaching the top of the head. Exhale out any stress or tightness, nice and slow. Repeat this five times. If the tightness or stress is extreme, blow it out forcefully, with the intention of releasing the stress NOW! This breath can calm and balance immediately. Repeat this breath many times a day, as needed. Relieving stress and minor physical discomfort by breathing is free, has no side effects, and can never be done too much!

Teach this breath technique to everyone you share Reiki with. Start every Reiki session you give with this breath. As they leave a session, remind them to practice the calming breath daily.

Blessing your food and water with Reiki

What we put into our bodies has a direct effect on our bodies: physical, emotional, mental, or Spiritual. Most of the time, we are in control of what we expose ourselves to, as far as food, medicine, liquids, and water are concerned. The choice and purity of those items are personal. Granted, the quality of our choices directly affects our systems. What we can be aware of is this: Reiki energy can purify, cleanse, and bless whatever it is we are about to ingest.

Quick experiment: Fill two glasses of water from your kitchen faucet. Let one sit on the counter. Place your cupped hand over the second glass, running Reiki with the intention to purify, for 30 seconds. Smell and partially drink the untouched glass first. Wait a minute. Smell and partially drink the glass infused with Reiki. Amazing difference! Why would you not infuse Reiki into everything you eat and drink and offer to others! Don't forget your pet's food and water too!

Reiki your home and office

Fill your home and office with the intentions of love, light, and protection. Daily infusions of the Reiki energy build, like charging a battery. Each infusion strengthens and amplifies the Reiki energy. Everything will benefit from the higher vibration. Your pets, houseplants, anyone in your space, and the space itself feels the comfort and love.

Those who do not resonate or who wish harm, soon cannot enter your space, or if they do, they don't stay long!

SACRED SPACE

Activate Your Reiki Symbols

Setting aside a sacred space for yourself at home is extremely important. This can be a room, a small section of a room, a chair in the corner of a room that only you use, your private space. Use this space as you begin your daily practice. In the space perhaps you can have an altar, for your sacred pieces, that no one else touches. This can be a small table, a chest, a drawer, something that houses, protects, and honors your personal items. As you begin and end your day, use your sacred space. This space allows you to tune in to your highest good body, mind, emotions, and spirit. Light a small candle each morning, to represent and honor your light for the day. (Be sure to blow out, or put where no harm can be done if left. Small tea lights are perfect for this, as they only last two hours) Activate your Reiki. Do your affirmations, Gassho meditation, and aura strengthening. Whatever time you have, five minutes to whatever time you develop for this practice. You are worth every second of this time! It takes 40 days to establish a new pattern of behavior. If you make it to 38 and skip a day, you must start over. After 40 days, this practice becomes part of what you do, without even thinking about not doing it. It will be like leaving the house without brushing your hair or teeth.

Sacred space can also be a private, secluded place in nature where you can connect to your highest good. You can go to this place in your mind when the weather or time does not allow you to physically be there.

As part of your daily practice, honoring the seven directions and elements is important. This practice is ancient, has been and is practiced by many worldwide. Setting a circle of intention and protection daily grounds and connects your spirit and your journey. The significance of the directions may vary with different cultures. Research and read other interpretations to find the one that resonates with you.

The following is one belief system: Calling in the grandmothers and grandfathers and guardians of highest good in each of the following directions, create a sacred circle of honor and protection. The North represents the mother Earth and abundance. The East represents the air and the ability to see from higher perspective. The South represents fire and transformation. The West represents water, sustainer and giver of life on this planet. Each of these directions can have an animal totem representing the energy and also a color. Now, the direction of above representing highest consciousness, Great Spirit. The direction of below, as above, so below, highest consciousness. The final direction is found within Self. We are each the final direction. Now, you are ready to greet the day!

REIKI CIRCLE

As a new Level 2 Reiki Practitioner, daily practice and symbol activation is important to continue to raise and strengthen your Reiki energy. Practicing on your family members, pets, plants, etc., is valuable and beneficial to all.

Joining or building a Reiki Community in your area is energetically rewarding and strengthening. Finding like-minded people with similar practices is comforting. We all learn from each other. Practicing with others, outside of family members, can be a huge learning experience and very different. Each person and each session may present new ways the Reiki energy heals. Remember: we are clear and open channels for the Reiki energy to flow to the recipient for their highest good of body, emotions, mind, and spirit. We are not attached to the outcome of their healing, as we do not know their highest good.

Reiki circles can be formed several different ways.

If you have multiple Practitioners, we have found it best to work one on one, or no more than two Practitioners performing the Reiki on the recipient. This means having several tables, if multiple Practitioners are present. If there are others without tables, chair Reiki can be done. Others can hold the group in Reiki energy domes of light.

Some Reiki Circles are open to the public. They can be done in your home (if you are comfortable) or at an office, or public meeting room that allows gatherings. These Circles can be offered for free or for a minimal fee.

We offer regular, monthly Reiki Circles as ongoing education. All Reiki students, all levels, are invited to attend. Everyone has the opportunity to receive, give, and share. Questions are answered. New information is offered. This can be the only opportunity some Practitioners have to work with others.

Many layers of healing can be experienced and discussed. Everyone benefits and grows in their personal practice and understanding of Reiki. A monthly "tune up" is experienced. There is a minimal fee charged.

PRACTICE, PRACTICE, PRACTICE!!!

Never minimize the healing energy of Reiki.

Daily embrace greater volumes of infinite, Divine, unconditional love.

CLIENT INFORMATION FORM

I understand that Reiki is a simple, gentle, hands-on energy technique that is used for stress reduction and relaxation. I understand that Reiki practitioners do not diagnose conditions nor do they prescribe or perform medical treatment, prescribe substances, nor interfere with the treatment of a licensed medical professional. It is recommended that I see a licensed physician or licensed health care professional for any physical or psychological ailment I may have.

I understand and believe that the body has the ability to heal itself, and to do so complete relaxation is often beneficial. I also understand that multiple treatments may be necessary to bring my system back into balance.

Privacy Notice:
No information about any client will be discussed or shared with any third party without the written consent of the client or parent/guardian if the client is under the age of 18.

Name: (Please Print)_____ DOB_____

Home Phone: _____ Cell Phone:_____

Address: _____

City, State, Zip:_____

Email:_____

Emergency Contact:_____Phone:_____

Are you currently under the care of a physician? ❑ Yes ❑ No
Have you ever had a Reiki session before?   ❑ Yes ❑ No
Are you sensitive to perfumes or fragrances?   ❑ Yes ❑ No
Are you sensitive to touch?   ❑ Yes ❑ No
Are you on prescription medication?   ❑ Yes ❑ No

Do you have any areas of concern?_____
_____

Signed:_____ Date:_____

Parent/Guardian consent if client is under 18 _____

BIBLIOGRAPHY

Bruyere, Rosalyn L. *Wheels of Light: Chakras, Auras, and the Healing Energy of the Body.*
    New York, NY: Fireside, 1994. Print

Dale, Cyndi. *New Chakra Healing: The Revolutionary 32-Center Energy System.*
    St. Paul, MN: Llewellyn Publications, 1998. Print.

Doi, Hiroshi. *Iyashino Gendai Reiki-ho: Modern Reiki Method for Healing.*
    Coquitlam, British Columbia: Fraser Journal Publishing, 2000. Print.

Eden, Donna. *Energy Medicine: Balancing Your Body's Energies for Optimal Health, Joy and Vitality*
    London, England: Penguin Group, 2008. Print.

Emoto, Masaru. *The Hidden Messages in Water.* Trans. David A Thayne.
    New York, NY: Beyond Words Publishing, 2004. Print.

Gerber, Richard. *Vibrational Medicine: The #1 Handbook of Subtle-Energy Therapies.* Third Ed.
    Rochester, Vermont: Bear & Company, 2001. Print.

Govinda, Kalashatra. *A Handbook of Chakra Healing: Spiritual Practice for Health, Harmony, and Inner Peace.* Old Saybrook, CT: Konecky & Konecky, 2002. Print.

Hart, Francene. *Sacred Geometry of Nature: Journey on the Path of the Divine.*
    Rochester, Vermont: Bear & Company, 2017. Print

Judith, Anodea. *Wheels of Life: A User's Guide To The Chakra System.*
    Woodbury, MN: Llewellyn Publications, 2010. Print.

Khalsa, Dharma Singh and Cameron Stauth. *Meditation as Medicine: Activate The Power Of Your Natural Force.* New York: Simon & Schuster, Inc. 2001. Print.

Lee, Ilchi. *Healing Chakra: Light to Awaken My Soul.* Sedona, AZ: Healing Society. 2005. Print.

Lubeck, Walter and Frank Arjava Petter and William Lee Rand. *The Spirit of Reiki: The Complete Handbook of the Reiki System.* Twin Lakes, WI: Lotus Press. 2009. Print.

Miller, Jessica A. *Reiki's Birthplace: A Guide To Kurama Mountain.*
    Sedona, AZ: Infinite Light Healing Studies Center, Inc. 2006. Print.

Orloff, Judith. *Intuitive Healing: 5 Steps To Physical, Emotional, and Sexual Wellness.*
    New York, NY: Random House, Inc. 2000. Print.

Pond, David. *Chakras For Beginners: A Guide to Balancing Your Chakra Energies.*
    Woodbury, MN: Llewellyn Publications, 2009. Print.

Rand, William Lee. *Reiki For A New Millennium.* Southfield, MI: Vision Publications, 1998. Print.

Rand, William Lee. *The Healing Touch: First and Second Degree Manual.*
    Southfield, MI: Vision Publications, 2005. Print

Stein, Diane. *Essential Reiki: A Complete Guide to an Ancient Healing Art.*
    Berkeley, CA: The Crossing Press, 1995. Print

Usui, Mikao and Frank Arjava Petter. *The Original Reiki Handbook of Dr. Mikao Usui.*
    Twin Lakes, WI: Lotus Press, 2011. Print.

www.ingramcontent.com/pod-product-compliance
Ingram Content Group UK Ltd.
Pitfield, Milton Keynes, MK11 3LW, UK
UKHW061140180426
11947UKWH00003B/16